Riverside Cemetery Association

Historical review of Riverside Cemetery Association

Cleveland, Ohio

Riverside Cemetery Association

Historical review of Riverside Cemetery Association
Cleveland, Ohio

ISBN/EAN: 9783337234096

Printed in Europe, USA, Canada, Australia, Japan

Cover: Foto ©ninafisch / pixelio.de

More available books at **www.hansebooks.com**

HISTORICAL REVIEW

—OF—

RIVERSIDE CEMETERY

ASSOCIATION.

CLEVELAND, OHIO:

CLEVELAND, O.
THE CLEVELAND PRINTING & PUBLISHING CO.
1889.

Board of Trustees.

ALFRED KELLOGG,	WM. SAMPSON,
S. W. SESSIONS,	WM. BAYNE,
F. W. PELTON,	I. P. LAMSON,
A. A. JEWETT,	L. SCHLATHER,
WM. WILSON,	H. J. COE,
A. S. GATES,	H. W. S. WOOD,
C. L. JONES,	JOHN DAYKIN,
J. J. CARTRIGHT,	J. M. CURTISS,
MARTIN SNIDER,	GEO. T. CHAPMAN,
J. S. HARTZELL,	J. M. COFFINBERRY.

OFFICERS.

PRESIDENT—J. M. CURTISS.
VICE PRESIDENT—S. W. SESSIONS.
TREASURER—F. W. PELTON.
CLERK AND SUPERINTENDENT—JOHN C. DIX.

EXECUTIVE COMMITTEE.

J. M. CURTISS,	J. S. HARTZELL,
S. W. SESSIONS,	MARTIN SNIDER,
F. W. PELTON.	

CEMETERY OFFICE ON THE GROUNDS.

"To Live is in fact to Die, and Death is the Gateway to Life."

"*The Grave should be surrounded by everything that might inspire tenderness and veneration for the dead, or that might win the living to virtue. It is a place not of disgust and dismay, but of sorrow and meditation.*"—WASHINGTON IRVING.

The Upper Lake and Bridge.

REVIEW.

BY THE PRESIDENT.

The high hopes and expectations expressed in our prospectus, issued at the inception of the Riverside enterprise, have been more than realized. Its phenomenal success has passed into and become a part of the proud history of our city. It is therefore with feelings of no little satisfaction that the Trustees, many of whom are among the founders, present this review of the history of the RIVERSIDE CEMETERY ASSOCIATION, representing the progress of an enterprise which in a little more than a decade has become the pride of our citizens.

Touching the inception of the Association, preceding any legal public action, there is an unwritten history, and between each line of recorded history there is an unwritten line, telling of anxious hopes and fears, of severe struggles and many discouragements. This undertaking, as many will vividly recollect, was no exception to the rule incident to the experience of men who embark in like enterprises. Riverside was the legitimate offspring of necessity. The Trustees of the city Cemeteries had reported the pressing need of additional grounds, urging the municipal authorities to take immediate action in the premises. The city had recognized the necessity, and by resolution had appointed a special committee to report a suitable location. But before any definite action had been taken, private enterprise had relieved the city of the heavy burden of taxation necessary to the successful accomplishment of the object.

Early in October, 1875, a number of citizens, in response to a public call and personal solicitation, met at the office of Judge Coffinberry, 201 Pearl street, to consider the advisability of organizing a Cemetery Association under the ample law of the state, and securing suitable grounds on the west side of the Cuyahoga river. We have no data enabling us to give the names of all the gentlemen who participated in this and subsequent preliminary meetings. However, on the fifteenth day of November the Riverside Cemetery Association was legally organized by electing the following Board of Trustees: J. M. Coffinberry, Francis Branch, F. S. Pelton, Geo. H. Foster, Diodate Clark, John G. Jennings, S. W. Sessions, Alfred Kellogg, Josiah Barber, L. D. Benedict, Nicholas Meyer, Thomas Dixon, Robert R. Rhodes, J. C. Schenck, Geo. T. Chapman, Elias Sims, Hiram Barrett. A. T. Van Tassell, John Daykin, and J. M. Curtiss. The Trustees immediately organized and elected Josiah Barber, President, and William M. Bayne, Clerk.

After the most thorough, painstaking consideration given to the work of selecting proper grounds. the Trustees were fortunate in securing the present desirable site of Riverside, containing 102½ acres, and combining, it is believed, greater natural advantages and better adaptability for the purposes desired than any other tract in the county. The services of Mr. E. O. Schwaegerl, an accomplished landscape architect and engineer, were secured to make a thorough topographical survey and prepare plans. The following April ground was broken, and the improvements were so vigorously pushed forward that on the 11th day of November, 1876. everything was in a condition of substantial completion—office, cottage. chapel and receiving vault: four rustic bridges, five miles of finely-graded driveways, and thirty acres of beautifully-lawned sections—and all in place and readiness for use and for the occasion of the Centennial memorial services.

Rutherford B. Hayes, Governor, and a large number of distinguished guests and citizens were present and took part therein. The exercises were appropriate and in the highest degree interesting, the ceremony of tree-planting being a novel feature and a pleasant part of the proceedings. The President-elect of the United States planted the first tree. Each guest and citizen to whom had been assigned a tree, planted it with his own hands, labelled with his name, and afterwards a diagram of the several groups and lines of trees was recorded, with the names of those who planted them, on the section plat of the grounds, thus carefully preserving the record for future reference.

Thirteen years have these trees budded and leaved since they were planted. Let us hope that they may abide in decorative beauty long after the hands that set them in place shall be folded to rest, and that when another centennial of our country shall be celebrated by our children's children they may rejoice in delightful summer shades and cherish endearing memories of the dead of Riverside.

Thus was Riverside Cemetery Association ushered into existence, but like all infant projects, it required long nursing and tender care ere it could stand, much less walk, alone. Of its early struggles and discouragements we need hardly speak. It is well that in the attainment of any great and worthy object we forget or think lightly of the thorny pathway along which we have trodden to success. It is well, also, that while the trials, sorrows and hardships of the past are thus softened and subdued by time, the future is kindly veiled from our view.

Of the twenty Trustees who started with us, and whose names are given above, eight now sleep beneath the green sod of Riverside. Nearly half of our original number, and two other honored Trustees, Mr. Thomas Lamson, who was indeed with us, if not of us, from the beginning, and Mr. John Bigelow, making ten Trustees who have surrendered their badges of office and life's duties within the few years of our organization. The last to leave his labors and this Board (for they all fell in harness) was our honored and lamented first President, Josiah Barber, who to the last counseled and worked for the enterprise he so dearly loved, and within whose sacred precincts his enfeebled body was so soon to find rest.

These feelings and events naturally cast a shadow of gravity over our deliberations which was unavoidable, yet we may feel and express joy and exchange congratulations at the success of the enterprise which has given us these beautiful grounds and placed the project on a firm financial foundation.

Nearly fourteen years ago we took these grounds fresh from the hand of nature, but with a heavy obligation to satisfy the demands of a fortunate middleman, (the purchase price being $102,457.00) and, after two years spent in grading and improving the ground, at an expense of several thousand dollars, we were enabled by reason of reduction obtained in purchase price, by raising the cash, and the liberal subscriptions made in advance for lots by public-spirited citizens, to bond the enterprise for $90,000. The bonds drew 8 per cent. semi-annual interest, and citizens interested in the enterprise were obliged to take them, as there was no sale for them on the money markets. The project was young, and, like most new enterprises, it was burdensome until firmly established and made a demonstrated success.

Starting with no endowment, and without receiving a dollar in donation even up to the present time from any source, (although a most appropriate object for generous action) this beneficent undertaking has not only beautified and maintained these sacred grounds, but wiped out over 25 per cent. of its entire debt. On January 1, 1889, the Association called in the $90,000 outstanding bonds. The sinking fund provided for by the trust mortgage given by the Association as security for these bonds and interest was, according to the terms of the mortgage, to receive two-thirds of all receipts derived from the sale of lots. These terms had been fully complied with, and on the day the bonds were called in the Association, out of this sinking fund, retired $20,000 of them. The remaining $70,000, which represents our present entire debt, was refunded at 6 per cent. semi-annual interest. As an indication of the public confidence in our enterprise, we are gratified in being enabled to say that every dollar of the new issue of $70,000 of bonds, which were to run from five to twenty years, at the option of the Association, was eagerly sought for even before the authority to issue was given.

To ascertain whether we were exhausting our available lands by sales faster than we were reducing our indebtedness, a careful computation of the sold and unsold lots has recently been made, and the results are most gratifying. Scarcely more than one-sixth of the lots have been sold, while the current receipts from sources other than land sales, which are constantly increasing, are nearly sufficient to pay the ordinary running expenses of the Cemetery.

Large, but judicious, expenditures have been annually made in beautifying and adorning the grounds, the more recent and perhaps the most noteworthy of which are the commodious dwelling near the Pearl street entrance, for the occupancy of the Superintendent, and a pretty and convenient lodge at the Jennings avenue entrance, securing thereby, through the occupants thereof, the much-needed accommodation to those visiting the Cemetery out of regular office hours, as well as affording better protection to the grounds. The present year has witnessed the displacement of two rustic bridges, and the erection in their stead, at a cost of $8,000, on foundations of heavy masonry, artistic iron truss bridges with firm hand-rail of unique pattern.

The signal success that has thus far attended our enterprise has greatly surpassed the most sanguine expectations of its promoters. Surely, the originators of Riverside, if they did not build better, built more opportunely than they knew. The wonderful increase of the population of the city in the last decade has far exceeded expectation. The necessity for extending the municipal boundaries so soon had hardly been anticipated. The two splendid viaducts now spanning the broad valley and uniting the once dissevered sections of the city were then wholly ideal. The improvement along the two avenues leading to and skirting the northerly and southerly sides of the Cemetery have largely increased the facilities for reaching it. Thus, by the co-operation of time and events unforeseen in its infancy, Riverside has been centralized and made approachable through some of the finest avenues and most pleasant drives in the city.

With judicious future management, it may safely be estimated that long before its debt matures the Association will have redeemed its bonds and accumulated a fund sufficient for the care and embellishment of the grounds in future years. To us and to our successors is left the sacred responsibility of zealously guarding the interests of this important trust, and as the ranks of the earlier Trustees and promoters, to whom this enterprise was so dear, shall be thinned by the hand of death, may their places be filled by those imbued with the same spirit of zeal and faithfulness.

OCTOBER, 1889.

RULES AND REGULATIONS.

INTERMENTS AND FUNERALS.

1. Whenever an interment is to be made, timely notice thereof must be given to the Superintendent at the Cemetery office at entrance to grounds. Persons giving such notice must be able to give the following particulars: *Name of deceased, place of nativity, late residence, date of birth or age, date of decease, date of interment, disease, name of parents or kindred, in whose lot interred, location of grave, name of undertaker, outside size of coffin or box; also place of death, whether single, married or widowed.* The same information will be required when remains are brought from other burial grounds for interment.

2. All graves must be opened by the Association, and all interments will be subject to the following charges, which must be paid at the time of giving the order:

For opening and closing a grave under five feet in length .	$3 00
For opening and closing a grave five feet and upward . . .	5 00

BRICK GRAVES.

1. Brick graves will be prepared by the Superintendent at the following prices:

Under three feet in length (inside) . .	$10 00
Three feet and under four feet . .	13 00
Four feet and under five feet . .	16 00
Five feet and under six feet .	20 00
Six feet and under seven feet	25 00

Larger sizes in same proportion.

2. An order for a brick grave should reach the Superintendent fully twenty-four hours before the time of funeral.

SINGLE GRAVES.

1. Single interments may be made in the sections designated for the purpose, at the following prices, payable when ordering:

For single grave under 4½ feet	$ 7 00
For single grave 4½ feet and under 5½ feet	12 00
For single grave 5½ feet or over	17 00

2. In these sections there can be no choice of location, as the spaces are filled in regular order, nor will spaces be sold and reserved for future interments.

3. Should any single grave be vacated and the body removed from the Cemetery, the ground shall revert to the Association, and the usual fee for disinterment will be charged.

4. Persons will not be permitted to plant trees, and no monument will be allowed in these sections except head-stones, which must not exceed the height prescribed.

No orders for interments on Sunday will be received after 3 o'clock P. M. of the day previous.

The burial of two bodies in one grave will not be allowed without special consent of the Superintendent.

The charges for disinterring are the same as for interments.

RULES CONCERNING THE CHAPEL AND VAULT.

Bodies may be placed in the vault at all times, but the length of time they will be permitted to remain will in all cases be determined by the Superintendent. The Association reserves the right of interment on twenty-four hours' notice to friends, whenever it may appear necessary.

Non-lot-owners, on applying for the use of the vault, are required to deposit with the Clerk a sum sufficient to defray the expenses of a single grave, burial and vault fees for the time stipulated. If such persons purchase a lot in the meantime, the amount deposited for single grave will be credited to their lot account.

Charges for the use of the chapel and vault are as follows:

For receiving and discharging each body $2 00
For vault rent for a person over twelve years (per month) 1 50
For vault rent for a person twelve years or under (per month) 75

These charges are doubled if the remains are removed to other cities or cemeteries for burial.

Burials from the vault will not be permitted on Sundays or public holidays. They are recommended for the forenoons of the week.

The remains of any person who died of a contagious disease will not be permitted either in the public or any private vault except when hermetically sealed.

UNDERTAKERS AND OTHERS.

Undertakers must so arrange the time for funerals as to arrive before sunset, in order to be out of the grounds before dark. On entering and while within the Cemetery, funeral processions will be entirely under the control and subject to the directions of the Superintendent and his assistants. Carriage-drivers, and others employed at funerals, must always keep on the drives, and remain with their respective vehicles during funeral ceremonies, and otherwise conduct themselves properly and in accordance with the Regulations of the Cemetery. No music or firing of volleys will be allowed within the grounds, except in the case of the burial of a military or naval officer or soldier. The Superintendent of the Cemetery is instructed to arrest any person offending against the above, or any other Rule or Regulation of the Board.

MONUMENT FOUNDATIONS.

Foundations for all monuments will be built by the Association. They must be six feet in depth, of the same size as the lower base of the superstructure, and level with the ground. The bottom of the lower base of every monument must be squared sufficiently to allow it to rest firmly on the foundation, as no wedging will be allowed. Orders for foundations must be left with the Superintendent at least one month before the erection of the monument, and payment made at the time of giving the order.

The charges for foundations are as follows:

1. For 20 cubic feet or less, $7.
2. More than 20 and less than 54 cubic feet, at the rate of 35 cents per cubic foot.
3. Fifty-four cubic feet or more, 30 cents per cubic foot.

An extra charge of one-fourth of the above prices will be made for all foundations built from December 1st to the following March 1st.

LOTS AND THEIR OWNERS.

The following Regulations are instituted:

1. For the better effect and beauty of the Cemetery, as well as of every lot.
2. They will greatly facilitate proper care and keeping, and reduce the expense of maintenance.
3. They are essential to the permanency of grave marks, and lot marks, as well as to the permanency of the monuments.
4. They operate to reduce the multitudinous number of insignificant monuments, head-stones, etc., and to promote the erection of larger, more becoming and more elegant structures, attended by less expense than the past custom of grave memorials.

REGULATIONS.

1. No lot or parcel of land shall be defined by any so-called fence, railing, coping, hedge, embankment or ditch, nor shall mounds over graves be allowed.
2. No lot shall contain any auxiliary vase, seat, rock or wire works, shells, toys, or any other architectural objects for which special permission by the Superintendent has not been granted.
3. No lot shall be decorated by its owners, or other parties in-

terested in it, with any tree or shrub, without special consent of the Superintendent.

4. Lot boundary or center stones will be furnished and set by the Association, at reasonable prices, as soon as a lot is sold.

5. Hitching posts or stones will only be allowed in places designated by the Superintendent.

6. Plans for all monuments must first be submitted to the Board of Trustees for their approval.

7. No monument shall be located upon any lot without consulting the Superintendent and receiving his consent to location, or placement of the same.

8. No lot shall contain more than one monumental memorial without consent of the Board of Trustees.

9. Neither head nor foot-stones will be permitted to stand or project more than twelve inches above ground. All stone slabs must be laid flat upon the ground. The Superintendent will determine whether or not a foundation for a head or foot-stone is necessary.

10. Wooden markers of every description whatsoever, being considered useless and detrimental to the general appearance of the Cemetery, are prohibited.

IMPROVEMENTS AND KEEPING OF THE GROUNDS.

1. The general care of the entire grounds and lots is assumed by the Association. This, however, does not provide for the special care of monuments, trees, shrubs, beds or vases of plants, etc., which may be placed on lots by their owners or for the grading or resodding of the lots or graves, preparing flower beds, setting head or corner stones, etc.

Estimates for any of the above-mentioned special work will be made by the Superintendent, at any time, on application.

2. No other person than the proprietor himself, or the proper officers and servants of the Association, shall be allowed to perform any work on any lot within the grounds, without a permit.

Proprietors may obtain such permits upon a written application, to be renewed annually. All such employes shall be under the supervision and control of the Superintendent.

3. The Superintendent will have entire charge of the planting and care of trees, shrubs and plants, in accordance with the general plan for the ornamentation of the grounds. Additional planting by the proprietors of lots, although not invited, may be allowed, provided, however, that the Superintendent approves of the trees or shrubs to be planted, and designates the location of the same.

4. The Trustees shall direct generally all improvements within the grounds, upon all lots, before as well as after interments have been made therein. They shall have charge of the planting, sodding, surveying, and improvements generally.

5. Private vaults or tombs may be constructed in such parts of the grounds as the Board of Trustees may approve, but a design of such structure shall first be submitted to the Board of Trustees for their approval, and a permit obtained. And in all cases the owner of the lot or lots shall be held liable for any and all damages caused either to the Association or to private property in the construction of either vaults, tombs or monuments, and shall pay in advance, if demanded, an amount deemed necessary by the Superintendent to remove all debris and put the lawns and drives in a proper condition.

6. If any tree or shrub standing on any lot shall, by means of its roots, branches or otherwise, become detrimental to adjacent lots or avenues, or for any other reason its removal shall be deemed necessary, the Superintendent shall have the right, and it shall be his duty, to remove such tree or shrub, or any part thereof, as in his judgment may seem best.

7. All persons employed in the construction of vaults or tombs, erection of monuments, or other work, must conform to the rules and regulations of the Association under the direction of the Superintendent.

8. Heavy-laden teams will not be allowed to enter the grounds unless by permission of the Superintendent.

9. No lots will be regarded sold until fully paid for, and if

parties make interments before paying in full for their lots, the Association reserves the right to remove the bodies to the single grave allotment, and to sell such lot or lots to other parties.

10. No sale, transfer or assignment of the certificate of ownership for any lot shall be valid without the consent of the Board of Trustees and their approval endorsed on the conveyance. The record of deeds kept at the office of the Association at the Cemetery is under the direction of the Secretary, and is the only evidence of the title of the proprietors recognized by the Trustees. Consequently, when a person receives a lot by transfer from a proprietor, he should send his deed to the Secretary at once to obtain the approval of the Board of Trustees, and proper record of same, for which he shall pay the sum of two dollars. No record of any person's interest in a lot, less than entire ownership, shall be made on the books of the Association.

11. All interments in lots for which certificates of ownership have been issued, shall be restricted to the members of the family and relatives of the proprietors thereof, except special permission to the contrary be obtained in writing from the Superintendent.

12. No further burial or improvement will be allowed on any lot against which there is an unpaid charge due the Association.

VISITORS.

1. Visitors will be admitted to the grounds daily. The entrance will be opened at 7 A. M. and closed at sunset.

2. No children will be admitted unless attended by some person who will be responsible for their conduct.

3. No rapid driving will be permitted, nor driving on the lawns.

4. All persons are prohibited from picnicing, from hunting or fishing, feeding or disturbing the fish, fowls or birds within the Cemetery.

5. All persons are forbid sitting, lounging upon, or otherwise occupying any private lot within the cemetery not their own.

6. Horses must not be left, unless fastened where posts are provided for that purpose.

7. Neither refreshments nor liquors will be allowed upon the grounds.

8. No person with fire-arms or dogs will be permitted to enter the grounds.

9. All persons are strictly prohibited from throwing rubbish on the avenues or any part of the grounds, plucking any plants, whether wild or cultivated, breaking or injuring any tree or shrub, marring any monument or landmark, or in any way defacing the grounds of the Association.

10. No person will be permitted to enter the Cemetery except through the entrance.

11. No person will be permitted to use boisterous or profane language, or in any way to disturb the quiet and good order of the Cemetery.

12. No money shall be paid to the attendants at the entrance or on the grounds. The entire time of the laborers regularly employed on the grounds belongs to the Association. Visitors and lot owners must not otherwise engage them. All orders, inquiries and complaints must be left at the office.

13. The officers and employes of the Cemetery having been appointed under an act of the Legislature of Ohio, special police officers, with power to arrest summarily all trespassers and persons who violate any of the rules and regulations adopted by the Board of Trustees, all persons therefore are reminded that the grounds are sacredly devoted to the burial of the dead, and that the provisions and penalties of the law, as provided for by the statute, will be strictly enforced in all cases of wanton injury, disturbance and disregard of the rules.

REMARK.—It is of the utmost importance that there should be a strict observance of all the proprieties due the place, whether embraced in these regulations or not, as no impropriety will be tolerated.

All well-disposed persons will confer a favor by informing the Superintendent of any breach of these rules that may come under their notice.

FORM OF DEED OR CONVEYANCE OF LOT.

All conveyances of lots shall be substantially as follows:

THE RIVERSIDE CEMETERY ASSOCIATION HEREBY CERTIFIES That...is the owner of Lot No............ ..in Section............................on the plat of the grounds of said Cemetery Association, in the County of Cuyahoga and State of Ohio, containing ....square feet; for which the said.. has paid the sum of............. ....dollars. And the said....................... ....heirs and assigns are and shall be entitled to the use of said lot in fee simple, for the use of sepulture only, subject to the provisions of an Act of the General Assembly of the State of Ohio, entitled, "An Act making provisions for the incorporation of Cemetery Associations, passed Feb. 24, 1848," and the several acts amendatory and supplementary to the same; and subject also to the conditions and limitations, with the privileges specified and contained in the Rules and Regulations that are now or may hereafter be adopted by the Board of Trustees for the regulation and government of their said Cemetery.

IN TESTIMONY WHEREOF, The said Riverside Cemetery Association has caused its corporate seal to be hereto affixed, and the same to be attested by its President and Clerk this............................ day of..one thousand eight hundred and.......................................

...., President.

.... Clerk.

THE NEW YORK
PUBLIC LIBRARY
ASTOR, LENOX
TILDEN FOUNDATIONS

A. J. Cartright.

BY-LAWS.

ARTICLE 1. Any person can become a member of this Association by purchasing a family lot in the grounds of the Association, and shall continue a member so long as he or she is the owner of said lot, and shall during such ownership be entitled to one vote for each fifty (50) dollars or fractional part thereof to the amount of twenty (20) dollars invested in lands of the Association, at all meetings of the Association.

ART. 2. The annual meeting of the Association shall be held on the second Monday in December of each year, after notice has been given of the place and hour of said meeting by publication for five days in one or more of the newspapers published in the city of Cleveland. At this meeting the Trustees and Clerk shall be elected, and to this meeting shall the President, Treasurer, Superintendent and Clerk make report of the business transactions of the past year. Any other business thought necessary may be transacted at this meeting.

ART. 3. At the first annual meeting twenty Trustees shall be elected, who shall be divided by lot into five classes of four each, who shall hold their offices for one, two, three, four and five years respectively, and shall elect a Clerk for one year. At each annual meeting thereafter four Trustees shall be elected to hold office for five years, and a Clerk for one year, or until their successors are chosen. All such elections shall be by ballot. All vacancies occurring in officers, committees, or Board of Trustees, from any cause, may be filled by the remaining members of the Board of Trustees until the next annual meeting for the election of officers takes place. Any extra meeting of the Association or Trustees may be called by the President, or by a call signed by a majority of the Trustees.

ART. 4. The Board of Trustees shall meet on the second Monday in March, June, September and December, and seven members shall constitute a quorum. The Trustees shall, within two weeks after each annual meeting of the Association, elect by ballot a President, Vice President, Treasurer, Superintendent and Executive Committee, and such other standing committees as may be deemed necessary to serve for the ensuing year, or until their successors are elected and qualified. The Trustees are also empowered to make all necessary rules and regulations governing the Cemetery not inconsistent with these By-Laws.

ART. 5. No Trustee shall receive any compensation or salary by virtue of his office as such Trustee, nor shall any Trustee, Superintendent, Clerk or other officer of the same have any interest in any contract work or material for such Association.

ART. 6. The President, or in his absence the Vice President, shall preside at all meetings of the Trustees and of the Association, and shall report at the annual meeting the doings of the preceding year, and perform such other duties as may be required of him by the Board of Trustees.

ART. 7. It shall be the duty of the Clerk to attend and record the proceedings of all meetings of the Association, Trustees and standing committees. He shall cause to be published, according to law, notices of annual and other meetings of the Association, shall solicit for the Association in the sale of lots, and shall sell the lots at the prices and upon terms authorized by the Board of Trustees, and shall keep a strict record of all such sales made by him, and shall collect and pay over to the Treasurer any and all monies due or coming to the Association, taking the Treasurer's receipt therefor, and of all orders drawn upon the Treasurer, of which he shall keep a strict account, and shall also promptly furnish the Treasurer the number of lots sold, and perform such other duties as may be required of him, for which services he shall receive an annual salary, to be fixed by the Board of Trustees.

ART. 8. The Treasurer shall have the custody of the funds of the Association, under the direction of the Trustees. He shall keep an account of all receipts and disbursements, and report the same to the Trustees at each of their regular meetings, and as often as they may require. He shall also keep an account of all sales reported to him by the Clerk, and perform such other duties as may be required of him by the Board of Trustees. He shall make no payment except upon order of the Clerk, countersigned by the President. He shall receive such compensation as the Board of Trustees may direct.

ART. 9. The Superintendent shall, under the direction of the Trustees, have the general care and custody of the grounds of the Cemetery. All improvements and work done on the avenues and grounds generally shall be under his supervision and care, and he shall engage and discharge all laborers and other employes on the grounds, and order and arrange their respective duties, unless otherwise ordered by the Trustees. He shall keep such books and registers, and make such reports to the Trustees and officers, and generally perform such duties as the Trustees may require. His salary shall be fixed annually by the Trustees.

ART. 10. The Executive Committee shall consist of five Trustees, of whom the President shall be one and ex-officio chairman. It shall, during the recess of the Board, have the same power as the Board of Trustees, under such limitations as the Board may from time to time prescribe, but shall submit to each regular meeting of the Trustees a report and record of its acts and proceedings. It shall be the duty of the Executive Committee to cause the books of the Association to be thoroughly examined at least once a year, and report their condition to the Association at each of its annual meetings.

ART. 11. All sales of lots shall be by contract or deed, attested by the President and Clerk, and seal of the Association, the form of which contract and deed, the terms and conditions of same, shall be fixed by the Trustees; but only the use of lots in fee, for the purpose of sepulchre, subject to the laws of the Association and State of Ohio, shall be sold and conveyed to purchasers.

ART. 12. The Clerk, Treasurer and Superintendent shall each, before entering upon his duties, give bonds in such sum as may be fixed by the Trustees, conditional for the faithful discharge of duty and honesty while in office.

ART. 13. Each officer, at the expiration of his term, shall turn over to his successor in office all books, papers, monies and other property in his hands.

ART. 14. Any officer of the Association may be removed upon charges against his character or official capacity, after due and impartial trial before the Board of Trustees, by a three-fourths vote of the same.

ART. 15. These By-Laws may be amended or added to by a three-fourths vote of the members, voting at any annual meeting of the Association, or at a special meeting of the Association, if such intended change is mentioned in the notice calling such meeting.

A TIMELY SUGGESTION.

In most large Cemeteries the thoughtful lot owner with means at command sets apart in his or her life-time, or in their wills, a trust fund placed at the disposal of the Cemetery Trustees for the perpetual care and adornment of their plat or lots. If neglect is not eventually to follow, this wise provision must certainly be adopted at Riverside.

TRUST MORTGAGE.

THE RIVERSIDE CEMETERY ASSOCIATION, OF CUYAHOGA COUNTY, TO THE SAVINGS AND TRUST COMPANY, OF CLEVELAND, OHIO, TRUSTEE.

This Indenture of Mortgage, made at Cleveland, Ohio, this 27th day of December, A. D. 1888, by and between the Riverside Cemetery Association, of Cuyahoga county, a corporation duly organized under the laws of the State of Ohio, party of the first part, and the Savings and Trust Company, of Cleveland, Ohio, party of the second part, as Trustee, witnesseth:

That, Whereas, The said Riverside Cemetery Association is the owner of lands containing 102 457-1000 acres of land, being the land conveyed by Titus N. Brainard to said Riverside Cemetery Association, and recorded in vol. 299, page 220, Cuyahoga Records.

That, Whereas, Said Riverside Cemetery Association, as it might lawfully do, has contracted debts for the purchase of said described property, and for laying out, protecting, preserving and embellishing the grounds and avenues therein to the extent and amount of $70,000.00 for cemetery purposes only, and

That, Whereas, In order to liquidate and pay off said indebtedness, the members of said Association being lot owners in said described property, did, at their annual meeting, held at the office of said Association, the 10th day of December, A. D. 1888, unanimously pass the following resolutions, to-wit:

Resolved, That the Trustees of Riverside Cemetery Association be, and are hereby authorized to issue and sell at par bonds of the Association, duly signed by the President and Treasurer, to the amount of $70,000.00, the proceeds of which shall be applied solely to the retirement of outstanding bonds; said bonds to run from five to twenty years, at the option of the Association, from the 1st day of January, A. D. 1889, and bear interest at the rate of six per centum per annum, payable semi-annually, and to be receivable at all times in payment for cemetery lots. Said bonds to be secured by trust mortgage on all lands and property of the Association, executed by the President to the Savings and Trust Company, as Trustee for bondholders," and,

WHEREAS, At a meeting of the Trustees of said Association held the 24th day of December, A. D. 1888, the following resolution was unanimously adopted:

"*Resolved*, That the President of this Association be, and is hereby authorized and instructed to sign and have properly acknowledged and deliver the trust mortgage authorized by resolution of said Association at its annual meeting, held December 10, 1888," and,

WHEREAS, in pursuance of said resolution, said bonds to the full amount of $70,000.00 have been duly executed, and are now ready to be negotiated and delivered, and described as the First Mortgage Bonds of the Riverside Cemetery Association, being a series of seventy bonds, consisting of seventy bonds of one thousand dollars each, numbered consecutively from "1" to "70," inclusive, bearing interest as specified in the aforesaid resolution, and payable at the bank of The Savings and Trust Company, Cleveland, Ohio, each and every bond, for its better identification, bearing a certificate duly signed by the President and Secretary of said The Savings and Trust Company, Trustee, as aforesaid, and that it is one of the identical bonds included in the $70,000.00 authorized by said Association and secured by first mortgage.

NOW, THEREFORE, Under and in pursuance of the aforesaid resolutions, and the power and authority thereby conferred, and for the purpose of securing to the holders of said bonds the payment thereof and interest thereon as the same shall mature, and in consideration of the premises, and the sum of one dollar ($1) in hand paid by the said Savings and Trust Company, said Riverside Cemetery Association has granted, bargained, sold, assigned and conveyed, and by these presents doth grant, bargain, sell, assign and convey unto the said Savings and Trust Company, Trustee for the holders of said bonds, and to their successors as herein provided, all and singular the property herein before described, with the appurtenances thereunto belonging, saving and excepting, however, from this conveyance, so much of the above described property as is contained in all lots heretofore sold by said Riverside Cemetery Association, and conveyed by deed or certificate, and also saving and excepting from this conveyance so much of the above described property as has been dedicated as right of way for the extension of Jennings avenue, by resolution of the Trustees of said Riverside Cemetery Association, adopted on the third day of December, A. D. 1877.

To have and to hold the lands, tenements and hereditaments hereinbefore granted, together with the appurtenances thereunto belonging unto the said second party, and its successors as Trustee on the trust, and for the uses and purposes and upon the condition herein provided.

Now, if the said Riverside Cemetery Association, party of the first part, shall well and truly pay to the legal holders thereof all of said bonds, principal and interest, to the amount and extent issued, as hereinbefore set forth, as the same shall mature and become due as therein provided,

Then and in that event this deed shall become void and of no effect; otherwise to remain in full force and virtue in law.

And it is hereby further expressly stipulated, covenanted and agreed by and between the parties hereto that the said Riverside Cemetery Association shall have the right and privilege, and the same is hereby reserved to said Association, to convey, when selected and fully paid for, to the purchasers thereof, such lots as have been sold and partially or fully paid for, but not selected or conveyed, such lots as have been contracted to be sold but not conveyed by deed or certificate, and all lots which said Riverside Cemetery Association may hereafter sell for cemetery purposes from out of the property herein described, the right being expressly reserved hereby to said Association to sell cemetery lots just as fully and freely as if this mortgage had not been made, and each and every such lot when paid for and conveyed by deed or certificate as above, shall, by the operation of such conveyance, be released and discharged from the lien of this mortgage without any formal discharge thereof, or record being made of the same, but in consideration of the foregoing right and privilege reserved to said first party, said Riverside Cemetery Association hereby expressly covenants and agrees to and with said second party that it will not sell any of said lots at a less price than thirty cents per square foot, and also that, from the proceeds of all lots sold while this instrument remains in force, it will cause to be set aside two-thirds thereof as a permanent sinking fund for the payment of said bonds and the interest thereon until the same are fully paid, and which fund shall, after paying the semi-annual interest upon said bonds, be safely and securely invested in United States bonds, or other first class interest bearing securities to the satisfaction of said Trustee at the end of each and every six months from the first day of January, A. D. 1889, if said surplus shall amount to the sum of $1,000.00 or over; otherwise to be deposited in some good savings bank, where it will draw interest, which said sinking fund shall, however, be at all times kept separate and apart from the other funds of said Association, and shall not, under any circumstances, be used for any other purpose than herein specified. And for the purpose of ascertaining the condition of said sinking fund and as to the fulfillment of said obligation by said Association, said Trustee, party of the second party, herein, or the holder of any of said bonds, shall have access at all reasonable times and hours to the records and books of said Association. And the President, Clerk and Treasurer shall make a full and explicit report of the condition and amount of said sinking fund at each and every annual meeting of said Association held after the first day of January, A. D. 1889.

And it is hereby further expressly stipulated, covenanted and agreed by and between the parties hereto that, in case default shall be made by said Association in the payment of the principal or interest, or any part thereof of said bonds as the same shall become due, or within ninety days thereafter, or in case said Association fails to comply with the obligations of this instrument as to the creation and investment of the sinking fund as hereinbefore provided, then and in that event said second party shall have the right, and is hereby empowered, at the request in writing of the holders of at least one-third in amount of said bonds, to take possession of property, and proceed to sell at public or private sale to the best advantage, but in no case at less than twenty cents per square foot, lots for cemetery purposes only, as laid out by said Association, until a sufficient amount shall be realized therefrom to pay such principal and interest thus in default, or to restore said sinking fund to the amount and condition it should be in, under the provisions of this mortgage, and for all lots thus sold by said second parties, said first party hereby agrees to make and deliver at time of sale a conveyance of said lot or lots in due form of law to the purchaser thereof, hereby authorizing and empowering said second party to make such sales and ratifying and confirming the same, and in case of failure of said first party to make such conveyance, the said second party, or its successors, are hereby authorized to make the necessary conveyance. The proceeds of such sales to be first applied to the payment of interest, and the sum then due and unpaid on said bonds, the remainder thereof to be placed in such sinking fund for the ultimate payment of the debt secured thereby. Or, if, in case of the non-payment of this principal or interest for the period aforesaid, the parties holding at least three-fourths in amount of said bonds so request, then the second party shall proceed by legal process to subject said premises to sale in the ordinary way of foreclosing mortgages under such directions as the courts may order.

It is further agreed that the Savings and Trust Company, Trustee, or its successor, is in no way made liable by any of the provisions of this instrument or by its undertaking herein, to any of the holders of the bonds secured hereby, except for willful neglect of some duty to be performed by it; and that, in the event that it shall become necessary to take possession of said property, as hereinbefore provided, or in the event that it shall be necessary to foreclose this mortgage, the said trustee shall be allowed, from the proceeds to be derived from any sale of the property herein conveyed, fair compensation for its services, including an allowance for the services of such counsel as shall be required.

IN WITNESS WHEREOF, The Riverside Cemetery Association, by its President, in pursuance of the authority hereinbefore recited, hereunto affixes its signature, and causes the same to be attested by the signature of its Treasurer and the affixing of its seal.

Done at Cleveland, O., this 27th day of December, A. D. 1888.
Signed, Sealed and Delivered in
  the presence of
        A. E. DAVIS.
        JAY COMSTOCK.
            THE RIVERSIDE CEMETERY ASSOCIATION,
                By J. M. CURTISS. President.

Attest: F. W. PELTON, Treasurer.

THE STATE OF OHIO, }
CUYAHOGA COUNTY, } ss.

Personally appeared before the undersigned, a Notary Public within and for said State and County, J. M. Curtiss, who is personally known to me as being the President of The Riverside Cemetery Association, and who acknowledged that he did execute said instrument as the President of said Company, and attached thereto its signature for the purpose therein named, and that the same is his free act and deed and his free act and deed as such President.

And I further certify that said instrument was attested by F. W. Pelton, to me known to be the Treasurer of said Association, and the seal of said Association thereto affixed in my presence.

IN WITNESS WHEREOF, I hereunto set my hand and affix my official seal at Cleveland, Ohio, this 27th day of December, A. D. 1888. JAY COMSTOCK, Notary Public.

The Savings and Trust Company, of Cleveland, Ohio, hereby accepts the obligations imposed upon it by the terms of the foregoing instrument.

THE SAVINGS AND TRUST CO.
C. G. KING, President.

H. R. NEWCOMB, Secretary and Treasurer.

[Recorded.]

The Rhodes Monument.

Cemetery Laws of Ohio.

AN ACT further supplementary to the "Act making Provisions for the Incorporation of Cemetery Associations," passed February 24th, 1848.

SECTION 1. *Be it enacted by the General Assembly of the State of Ohio,* That it shall be lawful for the trustees of any cemetery association, that is now, or may hereafter be organized under the laws of this state (in any county containing a city of the first class), to purchase, or take by gift or devise, and hold lands, exempt from execution and from appropriations for public purposes, for the sole and exclusive use of a cemetery, not exceeding five hundred acres in extent, three hundred acres of which shall be exempt from taxation. And it shall be lawful for said trustees, whenever, in their opinion, any portion or portions of their lands are unsuitable for burial purposes, to sell such portion or portions and apply the avails thereof to the general purposes of such association: provided upon such sales being made, the lands so sold shall be returned by said trustees to the auditor of the proper county, to be by him placed upon the grand duplicate for taxation.

SEC. 2. Be it further enacted, that all the receipts and income of such association, whether derived from the sale of lots, from donation or otherwise, shall be applied to the payment of the purchase of said lands, to the laying out, preserving, protecting and embellishing the cemetery and the avenues within the same, to the erection of such buildings as may be necessary, and to the general purposes of such association, and no debts shall be contracted in anticipation of future receipts, except for the original purchase of the land, and the laying out, enclosing and embellishing the grounds and avenues therein, provided no part of the proceeds of lands sold, or any of the funds of any such an association shall ever be divided to its stockholders or lot owners, but all its funds shall be used exclusively for the purpose of such association, as herein above specified, or invested in a fund, the income of which shall be used and appropriated as aforesaid.

SEC. 3. This act shall take effect from and after its passage.

A. J. CUNNINGHAM,
Speaker of the House of Representatives.

J. C. LEE,
President of the Senate.

Passed April 6th, 1870.

UNITED STATES OF AMERICA, OHIO,
Office of the Secretary of State.

I, ISAAC R. SHERWOOD, Secretary of State of the State of Ohio, do hereby certify that the foregoing is a true copy of an act therein named, passed by the General Assembly of the State of Ohio, on the 6th day of April, A. D. 1870, taken from the original rolls on file in this office.

In testimony whereof, I have hereunto subscribed my name, and affixed the Seal of this office, at Columbus, the 8th day of April, A. D. 1870.

[Seal.]   ISAAC R. SHERWOOD,

                                                 Secretary of State.

AN ACT Making Provisions for the Incorporation of Cemetery Associations, Passed February 24, 1848.

SEC. 1. Be it enacted by the General Assembly of the State of Ohio, That from and after the passage of this Act it shall be lawful for any number of persons, not less than ten, who are residents of the county in which they desire to form themselves into an association, to form themselves into a "Cemetery Association," and to elect any number of their members, not less than three (3), to serve as trustees, and one member as Clerk, who shall continue in office during the pleasure of the society. All such elections shall take place at a meeting of a majority of the members of such association, and after notice of at least 20 days in newspaper, or by posting at least three (3) written notices at public places in the township.

SEC. 2. That the Clerk hereinafter to be appointed shall forthwith make out a true record of the proceedings of the meetings, provided for by the first (1) section of this Act, certify and deliver the same to the Recorder of the county in which such meeting shall be held, together with the name by which such association desires to be known; and it shall be the duty of each County Recorder in the State, immediately upon the receipt of such certified statement, to record the same in a book, to be by him provided for that purpose, at the expense of the county, and the Recorder shall be entitled to the same fee for his services as he is entitled to demand for other similar services; and from and after making such record by the County Recorder, the said trustees and their associated members and successors shall be invested with the powers, privileges and immunities incident to aggregate corporations; and a certified transcript of the record herein authorized to be made by the County Recorder shall be deemed and taken in all courts and places whatsoever within the State as conclusive evidence of the existence of such cemetery association.

SEC. 3. That the trustees who may be appointed under the provisions of the first section of this act shall have perpetual succession, and shall be capable in law of contracting, and of prosecuting and defending suits at law and in equity, and where suits shall be brought against said incorporation, mesne process against it may be secured by leaving an attested copy thereof with one of the trustees, at least ten days before return day thereof.

SEC. 4. All such associations shall have power to prescribe the terms on which members may be admitted, the number of its trustees and other officers, subject to the limitations set forth in the first section of this act, and time and manner of their election or appointment, and the time and place of meeting for the trustees and for the association, and to pass all such other by-laws as may be necessary for the good government of such association, and not inconsistent with this or any other statute of the State, nor in violation of the Constitution.

SEC. 5. Such association shall be authorized to purchase, or to take by gift or devise, and hold land exempt from execution and from any appropriation to public purposes, for the sole purposes of a cemetery, not exceeding one hundred acres, which shall be exempt from taxation, if used exclusively for burial purposes, and in no wise with a view to profit. After paying for such land, all the future receipts and income of such association, whether from the sale of lots, from donations or otherwise, shall be applied exclusively to laying out, preserving, protecting and embellishing the cemetery, and the avenues leading thereto, and in the erection of such building or buildings as may be necessary for the cemetery purposes, and to paying the necessary expenses of the association.

No debts shall be contracted in anticipation of any future receipts, except for originally purchasing, laying out, inclosing and embellishing the grounds and avenues, for which a debt or debts may be contracted not exceeding $10,000 in the whole, to be paid out of future receipts; and such association shall have power to adopt such rules and regulations as they shall deem expedient for disposing of and for conveying burial lots.

SEC. 6. Burial lots sold by such association shall be for the sole purpose of interment, and shall be subject to the rules prescribed by the association, and shall be exempt from taxation, execution, attachment or any other claim, lien or process whatsoever, if used exclusively for burial purposes, and in no wise with a view to profit.

SEC. 7. All such associations shall cause a plan of their grounds and of the lots by them laid out, to be made and recorded, such lots to be numbered by regular consecutive numbers; and shall have power to inclose, improve and adorn the grounds and avenues, to erect buildings for the use of the association, and to prescribe rules for the inclosing and adorning of lots, and for erecting monuments in the cemetery; and to prohibit any use, division, improvement or adornment of a lot, which they may deem improper. An annual exhibit shall be made of the affairs of the association.

SEC. 8. Any person who shall wilfully destroy, mutilate, deface, injure or remove any tomb, monument or grave stone, or other structure placed in any cemetery, or any fence, railing or other work for the protection or ornament of a cemetery or tomb, monument or grave stone, or other structure aforesaid, or of any cemetery lot within a cemetery, or shall wilfully destroy, cut, break or injure any tree, shrub or plant within the limits of a cemetery, shall be deemed guilty of a misdemeanor, and shall upon conviction thereof, before any court of competent jurisdiction, be punished by a fine not less than five dollars nor more than five hundred dollars, and imprisonment in the county jail for a term not less than one nor more than thirty days, according to the nature and aggravation of the offense, and such offender shall also be liable in an action of trespass, in the name of said association, to pay all such damages as have been occasioned by his unlawful act or acts; which wrong, when recovered, shall be applied to the reparation and restoration of the property destroyed or injured as above, and in all prosecutions and suits under this act, members of this association shall be competent witnesses.

SEC. 9. Nothing herein contained shall be so construed as to prevent the General Assembly from exercising the right to bar such property at any time hereafter.

Observations and Suggestions.

BY THE SUPERINTENDENT.

The plan adopted by our Association of allowing but one monument to each burial plot, and dispensing with all inclosures, save corner stones, is most commendable. At the time of opening our grounds, this feature was in marked contrast with the custom then in vogue in our other city cemeteries, yet, in the main, this new departure has been received with a hearty welcome by nearly all who have rightly understood the motives actuating us. The rule prohibiting grave-mounds and head-stones, at first met with some opposition. Through lack of the necessary confidence on the part of its patrons, the Association was forced by public sentiment to generally allow both mounds and head-stones of limited height. A goodly number of our lot owners, however, chose to accept the plan without delay, and cheerfully dispensed with mounds. The improved appearance of their lots was so noticeable that soon, in order to meet the wishes of the majority, all grave-mounds throughout our grounds were leveled. This was a grand transition. The lawns, which had been among the early leading features of Riverside, were thereby quite restored to their original exceptional beauty.

With regard to grave markers, although the change proposed has not been so rapid and complete, we are pleased to note the steady growth of the sentiment in favor of the horizontal stone. In commending this, we are reminded that the slab lying above the coffined form is undoubtedly the earliest type assumed by the Christian monument, when marking the grave of the loved one, and it seems the most natural and expressive, marking, as it does, the site consecrated more exactly than the erect stone. Its inscription can be easily read by those who stand beside the grave, and the fact that it is invisible at a distance may be counted a merit, as every hint at ostentation is thus avoided. Memory recalls the names of many famous men whose tombs are thus marked in those cemeteries of the Old World after which ours was patterned. There is a Christian humility and dignity, a simple pathos in the aspect of a stone like the one here pictured, which is measurably lost even in the most modest vertical stone; and, viewed from a point of repose and sanctity so essential to every cemetery, flat stones are infinitely preferable to all others. When, by rule of the Association, these become universal, then will many of our lots be freed from the appearance of miniature stone yards, and the general aspect of the grounds be much improved. The erect headstones are usually unnecessarily expensive, and not in accord with the lawn plan; and when the purchasers have passed away, unsightly legacies will necessarily be left to the care of the Association. In order to protect and perpetuate the present charms of Riverside, we must carefully guard against further breaches of good taste.

MONUMENTS.

As our Rules and Regulations extend to our lot owners almost unlimited freedom in the selection of monuments, a word of caution against a very common error may not come amiss. Too frequently do we find in most cemeteries structures of the same style and proportions erected in close proximity. In many cases where the original design possessed peculiar merit, the very fact of its having been duplicated not only robs it of its chief charm, and reduces it to mediocrity, but adds to the grounds an air of monotony which, in Riverside, we trust will ever be wanting. Perfect uniformity in the designs of monuments reflects unfavorably upon the good taste and genius of their builders. Variety in material and design is most desirable, and it would surely be pleasing to all concerned if henceforth every monument erected in these grounds were wholly unlike all its predecessors. Better content ourselves with the plain slab marker for the grave of those we love, than to trespass upon the feelings of others by duplicating their memorials. People frequently have peculiar ideas about monuments, and often endeavor to secure designs that will, to them at least, illustrate some characteristic of the deceased, and in their selection of a design, they frequently find their ideal in some monument already erected. Their natural impulse is to duplicate the admired design, without considering that their memorial will then possess no individuality. Dealers capable of producing the best work are, as a rule, originators and not copyers, and it is therefore often safer to trust to their judgment than to rely on individual preferences. There is a growing desire for a better class of monumental work, possessing not only beauty and symmetry, but originality. This sentiment should be encouraged, and to this end I would suggest that the Association form a collection of rare books of designs for monuments and tombs, to be kept at the office of the Association, for reference both by lot owners and those who may at any future time desire to erect structures as memorials to their dead.

TREES AND SHRUBS.

Realizing the great extent to which trees and shrubs planted from time to time will necessarily affect the future appearance of our grounds, and feeling duly solicitous for their beauty, with a view chiefly of adding a pleasing variety of such only as are appropriate and desirable, the appended abridged list is herewith submitted:

TREES AND SHRUBS SUITABLE FOR CEMETERIES.

DECIDUOUS TREES.

Cherry—Double flowering.
Weeping Ash.
Gold-barked Weeping Ash.
Purple-leaved Beech
Copper-leaved Beech.
Weeping Beech.
Cut-leaved Weeping Birch.
Purple-leaved Birch.
Weeping Birch, *Elegans Pendula* and *Young's Weeping*.
Gingko.
Dogwood.

Horse Chestnut—Dwarf.
Koelreuteria.
Virgilia Lutea, or Yellow Wood.
Pinus cembro.
Weeping Linden.
Magnolia—Chinese varieties.
Pyramidal Oak.
Weeping Mountain Ash.
Cut-leaved Sumac.
Japan Sophora.
Sweet Gum.
Japanese Maple.

Willows, for obvious reasons, are not desired.

SHRUBS.

Azalias.
Althea—all varieties.
Dwarf Flowering Almond.
Purple-leaved Berberry, Thunbergii.
Deutzia—all varieties.
Hydrangea Paniculata Grandiflora.
Mahonia.
Tree Pæonia.
Forsythia.

Filbert.
Rhododendrons.
Daphne.
Upright Honeysuckle.
Japan Quince.
Spiræa—all varieties, especially Thunbergii and S. Van Houtte.
Weigela—all varieties.
Mock Orange.
Symphoricarpus.

Ampelopris Verchii (climber).

Full descriptions of any of the above named can be obtained at the office of the Association.

THE CLERK'S STATEMENT

For the year ending November 30th, 1888:

RECEIPTS.

December 1st, 1887, Cash balance.	None.	
From Personal Accounts for Lots	$14,327 06	
" Graves and Vaults	1,928 00	
" Receiving Tomb	640 80	
" Extra Work	537 17	
" Monument Foundations	235 13	
" Ice, $198.70; hay, $23.80	222 50	
" Interests on Accounts	150 44	
" Wood $3.00 and Shrubs $2.50	5 50	
" Recording Transfers	16 00	
		$18,062 60

DISBURSEMENTS.

Paid F. W. Pelton, Treasurer $18,062 60

In account with F. W. PELTON, Treasurer:

RECEIPTS.

December 1st, 1887, Balance	$ 2,694 63	
Received from Clerk	18,062 60	
		$20,757 23

DISBURSEMENTS.

Paid Interest on Bonds	$ 7,200 00	
" Sinking Fund	3,000 00	
" Labor (pay rolls)	3,708 49	
" General Expenses	573 55	
" For " Entrance Lodge," etc.	999 82	
" " Stone Walk	574 34	
" " Taxes	337 96	
" " Drain Tile	15 60	
" " Water Tank $20.00 and Pump $13.57	33 57	
" " Plants	17 17	
" " Sawed Flagging and Brick	146 11	
" " Perch Stone	63 50	
November 30, 1888, Balance in Treasury	4,087 12	
		$20,757 23

ASSETS.

Cash in Treasury...	$ 4,087 12
Personal Accounts.....	11,288 57
Memorandum Accounts..	165 55
Sinking Fund......	19,073 85
	$34,615 09

LIABILITIES.

Bonded Indebtedness $90,000 00

The sales of lots for the year. $17,261 87

Total number of lots sold (to Nov. 1st, 1889) 1,137
  "   Interments   "   "   3,393

N. B.—On January 1st, 1889, out of the assets, as shown in the foregoing statement, the Association retired $20,000 of outstanding bonds, thereby reducing the liabilities to $70,000.

THE SILENT DEAD.

" Peace to this Place of Rest!
'Tis common earth no longer now.
The gleaming sickle, and the laboring plow
Here cease their toil—for holy grounds
Are Gardens of the Grave—the bounds
"Twixt Life and Death—the awful bourn
From whence no traveler doth return,
Is peopled with dim mysteries—
The Spirit Realm around us lies!
Peace to these shades! these hills and dells,
Where Silence, like a Presence, dwells."

Centennial Memorial Services and Dedicatory Exercises.

The Centennial Memorial Services of Riverside Cemetery occurred on the grounds of the Association, Friday, November 11, 1876, the special observance of the day being celebrated in the unique and novel ceremony of tree planting.

A large number of visitors were in attendance, and the exercises were appropriate and interesting in the highest degree. The great event of the day was the presence of President-elect R. B. Hayes, who arrived during the afternoon and assisted in the beautiful ceremony—the planting of the trees.

Guests arrived in large numbers during the latter part of the forenoon, by street car or by private conveyance, those holding special invitations meeting at the City Hall, where carriages, provided by the Association, were in waiting to convey them to the grounds.

At a few minutes after twelve o'clock, Mr. Josiah Barber, the President of the Association, called the meeting to order on the beautiful mound which is to be decorated with a fountain, at the lower end of Centennial avenue, and where a temporary platform had been provided for the accommodation of the speakers. He introduced the Rev. S. H. Lee, of the Detroit street Congregational Church, who offered fervent prayer, asking the blessing of Heaven on the new enterprise. At the close of the prayer, the Arion Quartette sang the following hymn:

We meet not now where pillar'd aisles,
In long and dim perspective fade ;
No dome, by human hands uprear'd,
Gives to this spot its solemn shade.
Our temple is the woody vale,
Whose forest cools the heated hours :
Our incense is the balmy gale,
Whose perfume is the spoil of flowers.

Yet here, where now the living meet,
The shrouded dead ere long will rest,
And grass now trod beneath our feet,
Will mournful wave above our breast.
Here birds will sing their notes of praise,
When summer hours are bright and warm ;
And winter's sweeping winds will raise
The sounding anthems of the storm.

Then now, while life's warm currents flow,
While restless throbs the anxious heart,
Teach us, oh Lord, thy power to know,
Thy grace, oh Lord, our God, impart:
That when, beneath this verdant soil,
Our dust to kindred dust is given ;
Our souls, released from mortal coil,
May find with Thee, their rest in Heaven.

Rev. C. S. Pomeroy was to have delivered the address of the day, but could not be present, his absence being explained by the following letter, which Mr. Barber read :

CLEVELAND, November 17, 1876.

J. M. CURTISS, ESQ.:—MY DEAR SIR:—I regret exceedingly that the accumulation of engagements at the close of a busy week will not permit me to go with you to-day to your long-deferred inauguration of the Cemetery. I kept the way open during two successive postponements, but now it is hedged up. I trust the weather may not hinder you this time, and that the results of your tree-planting may abide in decorative beauty for many a century.

With sincere respect, yours truly,

CHAS. S. POMEROY.

In Mr. Pomeroy's absence, Mr. Barber stated that F. T. Wallace, Esq., had consented to speak, and introduced that gentleman, who proceeded to deliver the following appropriate and interesting

ADDRESS.

Standing upon this field, now and forever to be consecrated to the dead, and to be adorned and made attractive for the living, we are inclined to search the records of the past for an example.

It is pleasing to find, in the history of man, an early and touching instance of that forethought and taste which impelled the Father of the Faithful to select and purchase the field of Machpelah, with the trees and the cave, as the place for the burial of his dead and the resting place of his posterity. "Bury me not, I pray thee," said Jacob, "bury me not in Egypt, but I will lie with my fathers. And thou shalt carry me out of Egypt and bury me in their burying place. There they buried Abraham, and Sarah, his wife; there they buried Isaac, and Rebecca, his wife, and there I buried Leah."

These are but natural expressions of human feeling; instinct, a spiritual impulse, surpassing belief and disdaining question. It is a sentiment possessed by every nation, tribe and human being. Love of country, and to be buried with our kindred, are the ruling passions and the last expressed desires of the human soul.

A few years since, a young man, with his wife and little two-year-old boy, left the green hills of New England to make their home upon the great prairie of Illinois. One night the Angel of Death hovered over the new home, and spread his sable mantle over the child. Where they should make his grave, was a sad question. The grave of one little child upon the boundless prairie would be loneliness itself—a flower dropt in the middle of the ocean. Besides, they were not permanently settled, and could not brook the thought of forsaking the grave of their child. The spiritual impulse came to their relief. Taking up the little coffin, they journeyed back to New England, and buried their first-born beside the graves of the grandfather and grandmother, in the old church-yard. Then, with saddened, but peaceful hearts, they returned, gathered up the little garments and playthings to be cherished as sorrowful mementos, and made their new home beyond the Mississippi.

Who shall scoff at the nations which inherit, in common with ours, one of the noblest impulses of the human heart? Let the bones of Joseph be carried up out of Egypt; let the Chinaman return to the tomb of his ancestors in the valleys of the great rivers; let the dead student from Japan be tenderly carried back to rest under the shadow of the peerless mountain, and let the children of America hold in sacred remembrance and veneration the fields and sepulchres where their forefathers and kindred sleep.

In the presence of those here assembled, it would be superfluous to dwell upon the features of attractive loveliness of this field for the place of sepulchre, or to commend the enlightened judgment and admirable taste of the gentlemen of the Association who selected and purchased it, and under whose charge this important enterprise now is; for, in my judgment, it requires no stretch of the imagination to conceive that upon that third day of the creation, when the waters were gathered together unto one place, and the dry land appeared, and God saw that it was good, the appreciating eye of Deity, looking out from the windows of heaven, first rested upon the landscape of Riverside.

It is among the sadly pleasant memories of my life that I saw the "Old Man Eloquent" laid in his granite vault at Quincy; that I have stood at the tomb of Webster, by the side of the great ocean which he loved so well; have lingered among the primeval trees at Mount Auburn, which shade the mortal remains of the matchless Choate; have lamented Douglass, while standing by his ashes at Cottage Grove; and have dropped a sympathetic tear upon the grave of Lincoln, in the heart of the great prairie; but, among all the cherished places of the dead. I know of none where the aspects of nature combine in greater variety, or present more exquisite beauties, than your own chosen Riverside.

A plateau overlooking a winding river, in a valley hollowed out in remote ages by the surges of an inland sea; ravines which were once estuaries, but now woody dells, with copious springs for lakelets and fountains, and a rock of wonderful proportions, but foreign to its present bed, having migrated hither from its home in the Arctic mountains when Time was young—in the day when "God stood and measured the earth, and the everlasting mountains were scattered, the perpetual hills did bow."

There are sermons in stones to those who can read them. O, if that granite boulder, standing solitary and alone in the valley, could be endowed with the gift and power of utterance—could rise up and cry out—the mystery of creation would be solved. The elder Herschel, when asked by his son what, in his opinion, was the oldest thing in the world, picked up a pebble, saying, "There, my child, is the oldest of all the things that I certainly know." When visitors shall get bewildered in the windings and turnings in the ravines of Riverside, and shall come upon the great boulder to which allusion is here made, they may know thereby that they are hard by the chapel on the plateau—in the DELL OF THE ROCK.

Probably all great cities have some special points of attraction, either of parks, avenues or cemeteries. Cleveland is favored in all; but in none will there be in all time so much of individual and municipal pride as in Lakeview and Riverside. It is no disparagement to their colleagues and coadjutors to say that J. H. Wade and J. M. Curtiss are especially recognized as the projectors of the respective enterprises, and for their forethought and cultured taste. generations to come will honor their memory.

This delightful abode of the dead will, in all coming time, be anticipated by the living with cheerful resignation, and all who hope to rest here will be inspired to so live toward man and God that when the summons comes each will lie down in death as one "who wraps the drapery of his couch about him, and lies down to pleasant dreams."

In expressing our admiration of that modern taste manifested in adorning the homes of the dead, we should not forget our kindred who sleep in the cheerless village church-yard, or on the barren and neglected knoll by the country way-side. They are intimately associated with the earliest sorrows of childhood, and the bereavements of maturer years. They are sacred as places consecrated to our early dead—shrines to which we make pilgrimage in after years when all in the old neighborhood have forgotten us.

The scholar may revisit his Alma Mater in the venerable halls of Yale, or in the classic shades of Harvard; he may strive to awaken youthful associations with Livy and Virgil; he may read anew Æschylus and Xenophon, and reflect upon the pages of Thucydides, but the sacred stone of the Caaba, the Mecca of the heart, lies further back in the dear associations connected with the lonely and neglected grave-yard where the forefathers of the hamlet sleep.

4. Schlatter.

At the conclusion of the address, the Quartette Club sang the following hymn:

> Fount of mercies—source of love,
>   List the hymns we raise to Thee;
> From Thy holy throne above,
>   Heedful of our worship be.
>
> Creatures of Thy sov'reign will,
>   At thy feet we humbly bend;
> Let Thy grace our bosoms fill,
>   Be our comfort—be our friend.
>
> Here beneath the sunlit sky,
>   With Thy gifts around us spread;
> We beseech Thee—from on high—
>   Bless these dwellings of the dead.
>
> Guard them when the summer's glow,
>   Decks with beauties, hill and dale;
> Guard them when the winter's snow,
>   Spreads o'er all its mantle pale.
>
> Here—when wearied pilgrims cease
>   O'er life's checkered scenes to roam,
> May their ashes rest in peace,
>   'Till Thy voice shall call them home.
>
> Then, O then—their trials done,
>   Bid them rise to worship Thee,
> Where the ransomed of Thy Son,
>   Join in endless harmony.

Mr. Barber next introduced Hon. R. C. Parsons. He said he had not expected to speak, and that, indeed, further remarks were unnecessary, after the very interesting and graceful address of his friend, Mr. Wallace. Nothing, he said, showed the growth of Christian civilization more strongly than the increased care and attention paid to the last resting places of the dead. All over our land especially, the most beautiful and attractive spots were selected, and adorned by loving hands, that the places of our final repose might be made pleasant and graceful to the eye, and death, as far as possible, be shorn of its terrors. No man, whether a professor of Christianity or not, could walk through one of our cemeteries, so richly strewn with sacred dust, and not feel within him a sense of profound thankfulness that this was not the end of our existence, but rejoice in the thought, like the patriarch of old when he said, "I know that my Redeemer liveth, and that he shall stand at the latter day upon the earth; and though worms destroy this body, yet in my flesh shall I see God." It was indeed a consoling thought and promise, that this body, which is sown in corruption, shall be raised in incorruption, and this body, which was sown a natural body, shall be raised a spiritual body. All over Christian lands the last resting place of the dead is called, and fitly called, "God's Acre." When we have passed away, this beautiful spot, now covered with green sward, will be the home of countless dead. It is a melancholy thought, and one calculated to sober the most heedless, that to this place must come the sacred ashes of the father, mother, sister, brother and little child. The old and the young must lie down at last together. Here in the warm and quiet earth they will rest together. The stars will look down peacefully upon them, the rain will rain upon them, the sun will shine upon them, and the dew will fall upon them, but they will heed it not. Let us humbly trust that we and they may so live, that at last, when we shall be called to our final account by the Master, we may be able to say, "I shall be satisfied when I awake in His likeness."

The guests then proceeded to Centennial avenue. Here occurred the beautiful ceremony of "tree planting," in which many of the guests took part. On either side of the avenue, and at other parts of the grounds, holes had been prepared, near which lay choice specimens of maple or elm, ready to be placed where it is hoped all of them will so long abide in decorative beauty. The avenue was adorned exclusively with the American elm. On its south side, the trees were dedicated to the trustees and officers of the Association, while the row on the north side was dedicated to prominent officials and citizens. At different points in the grounds groups were arranged, each one being dedicated to some profession, official collection, or the like, as will be seen by reference to the groupings hereto annexed.

The first tree was planted by President Barber, on the west end of the avenue, south side. Hon. Amos Townsend followed on the north side, and was in turn followed by Hon. R. C. Parsons. At the placing of the trees dedicated to Mr. F. S. Pelton and Mr. Diodate Clark, trustees, deceased since their election to office, Rev. S. H. Lee made appropriate and touching remarks.

Hereupon the planting became general, a large number of gentlemen guests taking hold and setting to their places the various trees dedicated to each.

Memorable among the incidents of the planting were the placing of the trees allotted to Mr. Francis Branch and Judge Coffinberry. The former, in feeble health and strength, with difficulty alighted from his carriage, and placed his tree, which we may hope to live as a memorial of his personal worth and virtues, and his substantial aid and patronage in the interests of our cemetery. The latter, Judge Coffinberry, unable to leave his carriage, from the fact of being crippled, was relieved of his embarrassment through the thoughtful courtesy and kindness of his good lady, who came promptly forward and executed for him his part in the ceremony.

At this point, a carriage arrived with Governor Hayes, accompanied by Senator Schenck. The carriage made the circuit of the plateau, and, on its return, was met by Hon. Amos Townsend, who, on behalf of the trustees, made a short but appropriate address of welcome. He thanked the distinguished guest for being present, and, in doing so, only gave utterance to the feelings of the trustees and the citizens at large. He referred also to the interest Governor Hayes had shown in the enterprise from its first being brought to his attention, especially in so well fulfilling his promise to assist in the planting of trees, which should alike commemorate the presence of the planter, and also of the centennial year in which the deed was performed.

Governor Hayes responded with a few remarks, distinguished alike by their brevity and point. He said that it was in response to a request of the directors that he had come, for the purpose of planting a commemorative tree, but in doing so he did not expect to meet so many, simply supposing that the officials of the Cemetery Association would be present. He then referred to the beauty of the grounds, and spoke of the ornament which the place had added to the city.

Mr. Curtiss then handed him a shovel with which to plant his tree, remarking, "I am sorry it is not composed of silver." The Governor responded that it was better as it was for the work in hand, and then went to work in a business-like way, tramping the dirt in and arranging it in a manner which showed that it was not his first experience in that line.

This over, the party adjourned to the office, where an informal reception occurred. The front and rear doors were thrown open, forming a passage way for the people to enter and pass out. The Governor, stationed at one side of the room, shook hands and received the congratulations of the eager crowds who pressed about him. His apparent enjoyment of the scene was more than equalled by the hearty appreciation of his anxious admirers. His departure from the grounds was the closing act in the scenes of this eventful day, one long to be remembered in the annals of Riverside.

The following is the appended list of groupings to which reference has been made:

CENTENNIAL AVENUE.

NORTH SIDE.	SOUTH SIDE.
Gov. R. B. Hayes,	Josiah Barber, President,
Hon. N. P. Payne,	James M. Coffinberry,
Hon. Amos Townsend,	F. S. Pelton,
Hon. R. C. Parsons,	Geo. H. Foster,
F. W. Pelton,	Diodate Clark,
Martin Snider,	Jno. G. Jennings,
Belden Seymour,	S. W. Sessions,
J. K. White,	Francis Branch,
Col. Geo. L. Childs,	Alfred Kellogg,
Thos. Axworthy,	L. D. Benedict,
Geo. E. Hartnell,	Jno. Daykin,
Wm. A. McIntosh,	Nicholas Meyer,
J. B. Allender,	Thomas Dixon,
Thos. O. Poyer,	R. R. Rhodes,
John Coote,	J. C. Schenck,
Geo. Doubleday,	Geo. T. Chapman,
Robert Cartwright, Roch., N. Y.,	Hiram Barrett,
D. S. Brainard,	A. T. Van Tassel,
T. H. Lamson,	Elias Sims,
Henry R. Hadlow,	Hon. B. R. Beavis,
John Todd,	Thomas Holmden,
Joseph Turney,	Wm. Edwards,
A. Everett,	J. M. Curtiss.
J. H. Wade.	

OHIO GROUP.

N. B. Sherwin,	Hon. Wm. Bingham,
Hon. O. J. Hodge,	Capt. P. G. Watmough,

CUYAHOGA GROUP.

Ed. H. Bohm,   Felix Nicola,
A. P. Winslow,   Capt. Frank Lynch,
Wm. S. Jones,   Wm. Fuller.

MUNICIPAL GROUP.

J. C. Weideman,   E. K. Hutchinson,
F. T. Wallace,   W. M. Bayne,
J. T. Watterson,   John L. McIntosh.

CLEVELAND GROUP.

B. F. Morse,   W. G. Watterson,
Wm. Heisley,   S. T. Everett,
T. Jones, Jr.,   A. J. Rickoff.

FRANKLIN GROUP.

Maj. C. W. Krause, *Anzeiger*,   W. W. Armstrong, *Plain Dealer*,
Edwin Cowles, *Leader*,   W. Scott Robison, *Sunday Voice*,
A. W. Fairbanks, *Herald*,   A. Thieme, *Waechter am Erie*.

JOURNALIST GROUP.

J. H. Kennedy, *Leader*,   M. Watson, *Herald*,
F. H. Bradner, *Leader*,   C. H. Gray, *Herald*,
W. H. Eckman, *Sunday Voice*,   E. C. Hardy, *Sunday Voice*,
Robert S. Pierce, *Leader*,   A. G. Bernard, *Plain Dealer*,
C. S. Crowfoot, *Leader*,   N. S. Cobleigh, *Plain Dealer*,
J. A. Spencer, *Sunday Post*.   Geo. A. Preston, *Leader*.

KIRTLAND GROUP.

In honor of the distinguished Naturalist and Scientist.

Dr. J. P. Kirtland,
Dr. G. C. E. Weber,
Hon. Harvey Rice.

CLERICAL GROUP.

Rev. S. H. Lee,   Rev. C. W. Cushing,
Rev. O. D. Patch,   Rev. Chas. S. Pomeroy,
Rev. N. M. Calhoun,   Rev. J. E. Twitchell,
Rev. J. C. White,   Rev. John W. Brown,
Rev. E. H. Votau.   Rev. F. M. Searles.

W. J. GORDON'S TREE.

Contributed by him, and planted west of Designers' Group, in Section 6.

The above tree, the gift of the gentleman in commemoration of whom it is named, is a choice specimen of the scarlet-leaved oak. It was brought and placed here under the special care of Mr. Gordon himself, and expresses to the Association his sympathy with, and fine appreciation of, the enterprise and beauty of their cemetery, and will, moreover, ever be, in its beautiful autumnal foliage, a souvenir of the tasteful culture of its donor.

FOUNTAIN CIRCLE.

On Fountain Circle are two fine specimens of the cork-bark elm, contributed by J. H. Sargent and Josiah Barber. Mr. Sargent's tree is on the north side of the Circle, and Mr. Barber's upon the south. These two trees represent respectively the valuable aid and services of one of our most efficient Park Commissioners, and the old and honorable name of the Barber family.

I. P. LAMSON'S TREE.

Single elm tree, opposite the Journalist Group.

CENTENNIAL GROUP.

JAMES SEARS,	EBENEZER FISH,
GEO. L. CHAPMAN,	THOMAS LEE.

CITIZENS' GROUP.

E. J. HOLMDEN,	ROBERT BLEE,
TAYLOR EMERSON,	NELSON PURDY.
CHAS. MCNEIL,	

BORDER GROUP.

A. L. SAUSMAN,	S. R. BRAINARD.
WM. H. TOWL,	

BROOKLYN GROUP.

HENRY INGHAM,	A. W. POE,
E. H. BUSH,	A. S. HINCKLEY,
T. N. BRAINARD,	SEYMOUR TROWBRIDGE,
HIRAM WELCH,	OZIAS FISH,
C. L. JONES,	C. S. GATES,
I. W. FISH,	L. C. PIXLEY.
RUSSELL PELTON,	

DESIGNERS' GROUP.

Named in honor of E. O. Schwaegerl, the Designing and Consulting Landscape Architect and Engineer of the grounds.

E. O. SCHWAEGERL,	JOHN D. CREHORE,
JOHN M. ACKLEY,	THEO. M. TOWL,
JAMES M. RICHARDSON,	ROBERT MCEWEN.

The Lower Lake.

THERE IS NO DEATH.

BY SIR BULWER LYTTON.

There is no death. The stars go down
  To rise upon some fairer shore;
And bright in heaven's jeweled crown
  They shine for evermore.

There is no death. The dust we tread
  Shall change beneath the summer shower
To golden grain or mellow fruit,
  Or rainbow-tinted flower.

The granite rocks disorganize,
  And feed the hungry moss they bear;
The forest leaves drink daily life
  From out the viewless air.

There is no death. The leaves may fall
  And flowers may fade and pass away;
They only wait through wintry hours,
  The coming of the May.

There is no death. An angel-form
  Walks o'er the earth with silent tread,
And bears our best-loved ones away;
  And then we call them "dead."

He leaves our hearts all desolate,
  He plucks our sweetest, fairest flowers:
Transplanted into bliss, they now
  Adorn immortal bowers.

The bird-like voice, whose joyous tones
  Made glad these scenes of sin and strife,
Sings now an everlasting song
  Around the tree of life.

Where'er he sees a smile too bright,
  Or heart too pure for taint and vice,
He bears it to that world of light
  To dwell in Paradise.

Born unto that undying life,
  They leave us but to come again;
With joy we welcome them—the same,
  Except in sin and pain.

And ever near us, though unseen,
  The dear immortal spirits tread;
For all this boundless universe
  Is life—there are no dead.

Riverside Grounds.

BY F. T. WALLACE.

The judicious selection of Riverside for a place of sepulchre, by the Association, met the cordial and prompt approval of the public while yet it was resting in its almost primeval nature.

When, after a few months, under the hand of the landscape architect and engineer, its possibilities for artistic development had been made manifest; when the woody dells had been made accessible, and rustic bridges had been built over rivulets and lakelets; when the broad avenue on the high plateau had been lined with trees, the hundreds of sections made green with fresh sod, and flowering shrubs waved in the breeze and saluted the sun, nature and art seemed to have united to honor the dead and console the living.

So interesting to moderns have these grounds now become that not only is their geological formation a subject of thoughtful consideration, but the history of their possession and occupation by prehistoric man is, in these days, no less a theme of anxious research and earnest contemplation.

The plateaus, the bluffs, and the woody dells which border the banks of the Cuyahoga valley, worked out in remote ages by the surges of an inland sea and the contending waters of the winding river, are the rich spoils of the battle of the ages between the contending forces of the Lake and the River, in which the latter triumphed—the Lake retiring, leaving the River in possession of the field, now the rich and beautiful valley overlooked by many delightful promontories, prëeminent among which are the grounds of Riverside.

Modern research has disclosed evidences of a prehistoric nation, the subjects of which were thickly settled throughout our own and many western states, who built the wondrous mounds along the borders of rivers, cultivated broad fields, and dwelt and worshiped upon the "high places" of the land. They occupied the plateaus

of the Cuyahoga during unknown ages, and departed therefrom
even before letters had been invented by man, leaving no monolith
or tomb carved with hieroglyphics to indicate to their successors
either their origin, race, or ultimate fate.

The primeval possessors of these grounds, we, for want of more
definite designation, characterize according to the remains of their
wonderful works, the Mound Builders. They were doubtless the
remote provincial subjects of the empire of Peru, or the ancestors
of the men who built the prehistoric pyramid of Cholula in the
valley of Mexico. Ours is called a new country, but we uncon-
sciously tread upon the ashes of dead nations.

After unknown ages came the Indian, of mysterious origin, and
built his wigwam upon these high places and pleasant outlooks, but
so far remote in time as to bring with him no legends of the departed
Mound Builder. The knowledge of his occupancy of these grounds
is yet within the memory of living men, supplemented by two hundred years of colonial history. In confirmation thereof, we quote
a paragraph from the address delivered at the dedication of South
Side Park:

"Two hundred years ago, where we now stand, Christianity was
taught him (the Indian) by the French missionaries, and from here
were written letters, now extant in the archives of France, to
Madame Maintenon, the wife of Louis XIV, descriptive of the
Indians, the forests and rivers upon the borders of Lake Erie, and
the first description on paper of the wonderful Falls, over which is
discharged the blue waters of this magnificent chain of lakes.

"Less than a year ago, I was told by an intelligent gentleman,
since deceased, who lived here in 1833, that when officers of the
U. S. Army were on their way to Washington with the Indian war-
rior, Black Hawk, a day was spent here to enable their captive to
launch a canoe and glide up to one of the bluffs just above here to
a locality which he pointed out as the exact place where the wigwam
stood in which he was born, and the grave of his mother. That
locality, as described to me, is the high bluff and plateau where the
river approaches nearest on the easterly side of, and included within, Riverside cemetery grounds. I asked my informant if the
savage evinced any emotion common to civilized man under like
circumstances. He said: 'Yes, every manifestation but tears; the
nervous excitement, the expanding chest, the quivering lips.'
Every phase of humanity was exalted, in my estimation, when I

heard that the Napoleon of a savage empire could turn aside from his journey to visit the scenes of his forest childhood, and a wild mother's grave."

The venerable Harvey Rice, author of "PIONEERS OF THE WESTERN RESERVE," who, on the occasion of Black Hawk's advent, was a resident of Cleveland, and who, though more than half a century has elapsed, vividly remembers the same, thus records the historic event: "It is a memorable fact that while the captives were returning from Washington, they stopped at Cleveland. Black Hawk remembered the place, and referred to the fact that his mother died in the valley of the Cuyahoga river, and was buried about two miles up the river on a high bluff, which he asked permission to visit unattended and alone. This he was allowed to do. He procured a skiff, seized the oar, and sped rapidly up the river, recognized the high bluff on which sleeps the dust of his mother—a bluff that projects into the valley from the south-east corner of what is now the Riverside Cemetery—ascended it, and there lingered in silence for an hour or more, when he returned and placed himself in charge of his custodian. In relating the story of his visit to his associates in captivity, it was observed by the citizens present that his breast heaved with emotion, and that a tear, though he was unused to weep, stole adown his weather-beaten cheek—a tear which he endeavored to hide by turning his face away from observation. The truth is, that Black Hawk, though a savage, was a man of heart. There was a touch of nature in him which made him akin to the civilized fraternity of mankind. The bluff which he visited had become consecrated ground in the estimation of his race, and should be crowned with a monument significant of its Indian history."

The last above statement fully corroborates the first, and puts historical truth beyond doubt; the only variance being merely as to whether the party was journeying east or west when the event occurred. The last statement is doubtless the correct one, as it is based upon the personal knowledge of the venerable historian.

The ever-living spring of purest water that trickles from the side of the bluff where once stood the Black Hawk wigwam, has quenched alike the thirst of the Mound Builder, the Indian and the White Man, and will continue to flow till the last of the present race shall be entombed in the thrice consecrated grounds of Riverside.

A Tribute to Riverside.

BY CHAS. F. OLNEY.

Said Tallyrand, "Show me the Cemeteries of a country, and I will tell you of its culture, its civilization." Were he to inspect the beautiful Cemeteries of Cleveland, our beauteous " Cities of the Dead," how high would be his estimate of the culture and refinement of the people of the Forest City.

The word Cemetery signifies a resting place, and Riverside is therefore but an exquisitely beautiful dormitory where our loved ones sleep.

As I roamed through Riverside a few weeks since, the virgin forests all aglow with the pink and scarlet rhus, the crimson woodbine, the purple oak, the golden chestnut and beech, the multicolored maple, etc., etc., as I turned into the paths along the calm, silver lakelets, in which the wonderful Autumn tints were mirrored, and along the banks of which the robins and the hermit-thrushes were singing their Te Deums, and then, as I rambled over the emerald lawns spangled with beds of fragrant flowers, I thought if the dead *could* speak, how heartily they would thank us for selecting so entrancing a retreat for their long sleep.

And why should we not set apart the most beautiful spots of earth for the ashes of our beloved? Let the hill-tops of the Silent City be kissed by the first morning ray and the last gleam of day; let dancing rivulets sing their glad hymns of praise: let silver lakelets picture the glories of earth and heaven ; let Luna and the starry host shed their hallowed influence upon the peaceful scene; let Flora contribute her choicest offerings; in short, let nature and art so combine as to express in our Cemeteries our highest ideals of beauty and harmony.

Among the varied attractions of our progressive city, few afford the weary soul the satisfaction to be derived from a drive or a stroll through Riverside. In the early morning, at the sunny noon-tide, in the golden twilight, this beautiful spot seems invested with so holy an interest that the "Gates Ajar" almost seem to open and reveal the brightness beyond. It is well for the living to pass often through the streets of the " City of the Dead."

> "Why should the memories of the dead
> Be ever those of gloom and sadness?
> Why should their dwellings not be made
> 'Mid scenes of light and life and gladness?
> Here let the young and gay repair
> And in this scene of light and beauty
> Gather from earth and sky and air
> Lessons of Life and Love and Duty."

LAID AWAY.

Come to the silent city,
  Enter its shadows gray;
On through its winding labyrinths,
  Reverently, slowly stray.
Hear the moan of the waving trees,
List the dirge of the sighing breeze,
Tolling its myriad memories,
  Hopefully laid away.

Dawn on the breathless city
  Heralds the coming day;
Floating banners of rose and snow
  Mingle with pearl and gray,
Telling how snow-white infancy—
Rosy flushes and beaming eye,
Still and cold and pulseless lie.
  Tearfully laid away.

Noon on the gleaming city
  Pours its refulgent ray,
Flooding alike the Parian stone
  And the pauper's nameless clay;
Telling its tale of manhood's prime
And maidenhood's radiant blossom time;
Hopes and visions and dreams sublime
  Silently laid away.

Eve o'er the shadow city!
  Autumn winds softly play,
Whirling the dying Autumn flowers
  O'er the pulseless clay;
Weaving the crown the just receive,
Telling of crowns the victor weaves,
Purpling clusters and crimson leaves,
Fruitful lives, with their golden sheaves
  Garnered and laid away.

Night o'er the dreamless city
  Steals with her shadows gray;
Silent warders on Heaven's heights
  Fold their white wings to pray;
Telling of pilgrims, travel-worn,
Quietly laying their burdens down,
Sinking to rest with the setting sun,
  And peacefully laid away.

IN MEMORIAM.

Of the more than 3,300 who, in thirteen years, have been laid to rest in Riverside, limited space will justify barely a brief notice of a few well-remembered names, including such of the trustees and officers of the Association as death has taken therefrom.

DANIEL P. RHODES

was born in Sudbury, Rutland county, Vermont, in 1814. When but five years of age, he lost his father, and from that time was compelled to help earn his own living. Almost at the threshold of life, therefore, he had to struggle with adverse circumstances, and was forced to overcome by his own energy the discouragements and difficulties everywhere met with. When he was fifteen years of age his mother remarried, and he then found a home with his step-father for six years.

At the age of twenty-one, he determined to leave Vermont, and make for himself a home and fortune in the distant West. His step-father was strongly attached to him, and, being a man of means, offered him a farm if he would remain in Vermont. But the young man was firm in his purpose, and, declining the tempting offer, left for the West. On his subsequently returning to the home of his youth, his step-father offered him half of his property if he would remain and occupy it. The inducement was very strong, but he had made an engagement of marriage with a lady in the West, and before giving a final answer to the proposition, he decided to revisit his pioneer home and consult her to whom he had plighted his faith.

He came back West by canal, and, on the long, slow journey, had ample time to consider the subject of his future home. The beauty and grandeur of the Western scenery, the freedom from all conventionalities which prevail in more densely settled sections, the stern, rugged virtues of the men whom he found in the wilderness, together with the independent career opened to him, impressed his manly mind, and he resolved to cast his lot in the West. Saying nothing of the matter to his affianced, he wrote to his parents, making known his purpose to decline their kind offer, and future circumstances proved the wisdom of his decision.

For thirty years Mr. Rhodes was a resident of Cleveland, and the same restless and indomitable energy which prompted him to prefer the untrodden paths of the wilderness to the pleasures of an Eastern home, accompanied him throughout that time, and impressed his name upon many of the most important enterprises of the Forest City. He was one of the pioneers in the coal trade of Cleveland, which has since grown to such magnificent proportions.

His first enterprise in that line was at what are known as the old Brier Hill mines, in 1845, in company with Gov. Tod and Mr. Ford. Their production of coal was about fifty tons per week, and this was then deemed a large business. The difficulties in the way of introduction of even this, the very best of coal, were very great. Wood was the universal fuel for domestic use. The only chance to sell coal was to the lake steamers, and even there the old prejudices against any departure from the beaten track had to be overcome. Mr. Rhodes, who had charge of the Cleveland end of the business, was, however, well fitted to make a fight against obstacles, and by his steady perseverance he succeeded in introducing coal largely for use on the lake boats. He was an untiring worker, ever on the watch for his customers, from early morn to the close of day, devoting his evenings to his correspondence, and other office work. The coal business of the firm grew rapidly, and the members turned their attention to other sections of the State, opening mines in both Tuscarawas and Wayne counties. In 1857 Mr. Rhodes formed a co-partnership with Mr. J. F. Card, and they went to work with great earnestness to develope the blackband ore and other mineral resources of Tuscarawas county.

In 1860 his attention was attracted to the mineral resources of Stark county, and, in that year, he opened the famous Willowbank mine, which proved to be one of the most extensive and profitable coal mines ever opened in Ohio. He became interested later in many other mines in the same county, so that from his original production of fifty tons weekly, he increased the amount until, at the time of his death, he had the controlling interest or was a large owner in mines which were capable of producing two thousand tons daily. His peddling steam-boat business of 1845-50 had increased under the direction of the firm, of which he was the founder, to a trade of two hundred and fifty thousand tons yearly.

He took an active part in the construction of the Northern division of the Cleveland & Toledo railroad, and of the Massillon & Cleveland and Lake Shore and Tuscarawas Valley railways. His residence was on the west side of the Cuyahoga, and he did more than any other man to build up that portion of Cleveland. One great cause of contention between the two sections arose from the persistent efforts of the people on the West Side to obtain improved means of communication with the more important region east of the river. In all these contests, from the time when a float bridge was the only means of passage, to the inception and partial completion of the splendid Viaduct, (for he died before it was finished), he was one of the foremost in urging the claims of his section of the city. He, in company with H. S. Stevens, constructed the West Side Street Railroad; he was a zealous promoter of the building of the West Side Gas Works, and was the founder of the People's Savings and Loan Association, of which he was the president at the time of his death. He was also one of the builders, and a large stockholder, in the Rocky River railroad, which connected the West Side with the favorite resort at Rocky River. He was a large real estate owner on the west side of the river.

Mr. Rhodes died on the 5th day of August, 1875.

JEREMIAH HIGBEE.

Among the first of the aged persons whose remains were consigned to the sacred soil of this beautiful cemetery—"God's Acre"— was Jeremiah Higbee, the son of a New England minister, to whom he was born, near the close of the last century, in a quiet hamlet, surrounded with the influences of a Christian home and a pious ancestry; and, from which surroundings and associations he went out to try his fortunes in the sparsely settled districts of one of the southern States, adjoining our own, where, for several years, he was engaged in private teaching, subsequent to which he entered mercantile life in this State, in which he was actively engaged for more than a quarter of a century, retiring from it to enjoy another period of more than twenty years of exemption from the cares incident to active business, surrounded by his family and relatives until the time of his decease (1878), at the ripe age of 86 years.

Although of a quiet and retiring temperament, and averse to display, his friendships when formed were strong and abiding, and the memories of his kindness, affection, charity and justness are indelibly impressed upon the hearts of those who knew him well.

For a large portion of his life he was closely identified with church work and the great moral reforms of the day, keeping himself thoroughly informed by diligent reading and observation upon political, social and scientific questions as well.

He met the trials and afflictions of life with manly, Christian resignation, having been called upon to part with children, and twice to bid farewell to an affectionate companion, and finally to leave his children, and also her with whom he had walked many years, to mourn his departure, being remembered by them as a faithful parent, a devoted husband, and a honored member of society.

BENJAMIN R. BEAVIS.

Benjamin R. Beavis was born in London, England, on March 12th, 1826. When an infant, his parents emigrated to America, and first settled in Brooklyn, Long Island. In 1834 his parents removed to Ohio, and settled in the then township of Brooklyn, Cuyahoga county. He received a common school education, and, after arriving at the age of majority, commenced the study of the law. He was admitted to the bar in July, 1851, and commenced the practice of law at Cleveland early in 1852, continuing in the practice until his death, which occurred on March 4th, 1884, a period of over thirty-two years of professional life. He was elected as treasurer of Brooklyn township, and afterward as justice of the peace, and member of the board of education of Brooklyn

In 1867, that portion of Brooklyn township where he resided was annexed to the city of Cleveland, and he was elected one of the first councilmen of his ward in the Spring of 1868. As a member of the council he took great interest in the growth and prosperity of the city, and was made president *pro tem* of its council. In 1870 he was re-elected to the council, and in 1871 he was by the partiality of his friends and without special effort on his part, nominated and elected to represent his county as one of its senators in the Senate of the Sixtieth General Assembly of Ohio. The iron bridge spanning Walworth Run, and the great Viaduct were built during his trustee and senatorship, and he was greatly instrumental in their agitation and construction. In honor of his services, he was appointed and acted as president of the day on the celebration of the completion of the Viaduct on December 27, 1878. As a member of the last city decennial board of equalization and board of revision in 1881 and 1882, he served as its president, and thereafter practiced his profession until his death on March 4th, 1884, after a short illness, his wife, a son and daughter and a brother surviving him. His progress through life has been the result of a continuous struggle with adverse circumstances, and he was what is usually termed a self-made man. Earnest and sincere in his advocacy of whatever he attempted, a good husband and father, industrious in his habits, considerate in his actions, a good, safe lawyer, and faithful to the interests of his clients and to the public, he won the confidence and respect of his neighbors, friends, constituents and all with whom he came in contact. He was laid to rest at Riverside Cemetery, on March 6th, 1884, amid a large concourse of friends and neighbors, giving evidence of the great love and esteem in which he was held by the community.

DAVID S. BRAINARD

was born July 27th, 1815, in Brooklyn township, upon the farm where his parents had settled two years earlier. Cleveland was then a distant hamlet in the forest, which he lived to see the second city in the state, and whose limits now embrace the rural home of his boyhood. He died April 26, 1880, having lived the life of a farmer, and won the confidence and respect of his neighbors. He sought no office, but was often selected for official positions, in which he served the public faithfully. He was township trustee in 1856-7, and treasurer in 1845, 1847 and 1863. He was trustee of North Brooklyn Cemetery Association from its organization until his death. Rural life was his enjoyment. He was a true friend, a genial companion, a kind neighbor, and an honest man. He was a liberal contributor to the advancement of the public welfare. A wife, a daughter and a grand-daughter revere his memory, and a memorial symbol of the solid worth of the man and an enduring monument marks his resting place.

REV. THOMAS STUBBS,

who was more or less intimately associated with the religious life of Cleveland, for half a century, was born in the beautiful hill country of England, town of Kendal, 1801, and died at his home in Cleveland, February, 1884.

He began preaching at eighteen, and preached his last sermon in the Franklin avenue M. E. church, about eight months before his death, making a period of sixty-five years in the ministry.

In 1832, in May, he landed in Cleveland, camping over night on the beach. At once he began his ministry, becoming a member of the then Pittsburgh Conference, from which was formed the Erie, of which he was an honored member all his life.

For a number of years he traveled the then wilderness, called the Western Reserve. Along the lake shore, and into the interior, as far as Youngstown, his name was a household word.

In 1848 he was stationed at the First M. E. church, located on the corner of St. Clair and Wood streets. During his two years' ministry, the church was greatly prospered. There, as everywhere, large revivals prevailed.

From 1854 to 1857 he had charge of the Erie street church, which has since removed to another part of the city, and the Mission located on East St. Clair.

In 1866, on account of his wife's health, he located in Cleveland, West Side, where he resided the remainder of his life. During this time he served East Cleveland, Ashtabula and the Bethel.

For a few years he was not in charge, yet he was vigorous in body and mind, preaching in various pulpits to the delight of the people. He was catholic in spirit, and beloved by all denominations. He was a man of rare mental gifts—of a poetical temperament—of noble thought—a great lover of nature and his fellow men. In his prime no man in his conference surpassed him in eloquence. He was a most ardent lover of his adopted country, and his voice rung out for the slave when it took nerve and courage, and when the applause often came in rotten eggs and stones. The war for the Union waked his eloquence and enthusiasm, and in the darkest hours his inspiring voice gave hope to the people.

He had great power over men in attaching them to him personally. Friends once, friends always. Beloved by all who knew him; a man of remarkable purity of character and life, traits that shone in his benevolent and winning face, and exemplified in his walk and conversation.

Of more than ordinary ability, clear and vigorous in mind, original as a thinker, fluent, graceful and powerful as a speaker, his discourses abounded in beautiful figures and bright, poetic fancies. Coupled with a brilliant mind was a big heart, that found expression in charity and kindness, which will endear him to thousands all over his extensive field of labor.

When eighty, he was able to walk ten miles. When eighty-one, he preached a sermon in his son's pulpit that, for enthusiasm and buoyancy, would have done credit to a young man—that for noble thought and elevation of sentiment would have honored a man in his prime.

The grasp of his mind ceased only as he ceased to breathe.

RUSSELL PELTON.

One of the earliest of Cleveland's enterprising business men and promoters of the commerce of the lakes entered upon his final rest in Riverside, in April, 1888. He was of English ancestry, which came to New England about the middle of the 17th century. He was born in Portland, Connecticut, July 20th, 1803. In 1821 he married Pamelia, daughter of Joseph Abbey, of Chatham, Conn., spent his early life in his native state, living for a time in Chester, Conn. He came to Cleveland in 1835, locating in Brooklyn, now embraced within the city limits. They had two sons and three daughters. Mrs. Pelton died in June, 1879. He established one of the first foundries in Cleveland, located on the site of the gas works, near the Union railway station, and where he made all the iron castings used in the construction of the Weddell House.

About 1852 he established a line of canal packets plying between Columbus and Chillicothe, and in 1865 retired to his farm on Lorain street and Denison avenue, now in the city, and was interested as a capitalist in the Northern Transportation Company on the lakes. He was an upright, thorough business man, an exemplary member of the Methodist church, and a man of broad and liberal sentiments. He died at the home of his daughter, Mrs. Czias Fish, in Brooklyn village.

FRANCIS S. PELTON,

second son of Russell and Pamelia Abbey Pelton, was born in Chester, Middlesex county, Conn., June 8th, 1833; removed with his parents to Ohio in 1835, they locating in Brooklyn, where he also remained until 1868, when he became a resident of the city of Cleveland.

In 1854, he married Miss Mary Knight, of Glens Falls, New York. Of this marriage were born eleven children, five sons and six daughters.

His name was prophetic of the man, for he was always "Frank" and open, genial and warm hearted, kindly disposed toward everybody, especially the needy and unfortunate, making firm friends wherever he made acquaintances.

He was strongly attached to his home and his family, spending with them as many of his leisure hours as possible. His life as husband and father is well deserving of imitation.

He was possessed of rare business qualifications, having good judgment, with an energy and "push" that overcame all obstacles and surmounted all difficulties.

He was one of the first to note the adaptability of Riverside to cemetery purposes, and was one of the first trustees of the Cemetery Association.

Full of enterprise and public spirit, he was always ready to do his part for the promotion of the general welfare, and his judgment upon what was right and just determined his action.

As a Mason and Odd Fellow he was a faithful and conscientious worker, and both orders will long remember his good deeds and mourn his too early death.

He died at his residence, in the city of Cleveland, aged forty-three years, loved and lamented most by those who knew him best.

JACOB GRAF,

a native of Germany, was born February 9th, 1813; emigrated with his family to America, May 31st, 1848; lived upon his farm in Rockport until his wife's death, which occurred May 11th, 1885. He then removed to this city and lived with his son-in-law, Hon. Chas. Herrman, and died January 2d, 1889, as a highly respected citizen. He left a family of ten children, of which six survive him.

MARTIN KELLOGG.

Martin Kellogg was born in Easthampton parish, Chatham, Middlesex Co., Conn., on the 16th of February, 1793. His ancestors were Irish, and settled in this country at an early date.

His father, whose name was Martin, was a native of Marlboro, Conn., having been born there about the year 1765. He was a man of great integrity and enterprise; was often called upon for advice and counsel, and, although not a member, was a constant attendant and liberal supporter of the Episcopal Church. He married Rachel Hosford, daughter of Dudley Hosford, of Marlboro, by whom he had six children, viz: Rachel, Martin, Joel, Alfred, Rechelsea and Lucy Ann. The latter is the only member of this family now living. Mr. Kellogg died in Easthampton in 1825. His wife survived him twenty-five years, and died in January, 1850.

The subject of this sketch received a common school education, and, until he reached his majority, remained upon his father's farm. He was then employed in laboring by the month, which he continued for four years. In 1817 he came to Ohio, and remained one year. Returning to Connecticut, he was married, on the 2d of June, 1818, to Laura Adams, daughter of Benjamin Adams, of Colchester, New London county. They at once set out for Ohio, in company with the families of Judge Barber, Mr. Watkins, Mr. Branch and Mr. Ansel Young. They traveled the entire distance with ox-teams, the journey consuming forty days. Arriving at Cleveland in July, Mr. Kellogg settled in Brooklyn, on the place situated on Scranton avenue. He immediately commenced clearing his farm, and, although subjected to all the hardships of pioneer life, was never discouraged. At the end of a comparatively few years he possessed a comfortable home, and on account of its location his land subsequently became very valuable.

In 1856, his wife died, and he was married on the 8th of March, 1860, to Mrs. Laura Walker, who died July 17th, 1863. He only survived her a little more than one month, his death occurring on the 25th of August following.

Mr. Kellogg was a man of staunch integrity and high moral character; an enterprising citizen, and one who took an active part in forwarding local improvements and the best interests of the community in which he lived.

Mr. Kellogg had four children—Alfred, Horace, Charles M. and Sanford B., all deceased except Alfred, the eldest.

THE NEW YORK
PUBLIC LIBRARY

ASTOR, LENOX
TILDEN FOUNDATIONS

HENRY JOHNSON BROOKS,

born April 30th, 1813, at Berlin, Conn., came to Ohio with his father at the age of six years, traveling with an ox team and requiring six weeks to make the journey. His father settled in Carlisle township, Lorain county, being one of the first settlers.

He was married to Abigail Hart, November 6th, 1832, the ceremony being performed by Rev. J. J. Shipherd, at Elyria, O., where they first commenced house-keeping.

Having learned the carpenter trade, he commenced business for himself; his brother Samuel, learning the trade from him, afterward became his partner.

Their first important contract was the building of the Presbyterian Church in that place, which at the time was one of the finest structures in the State.

Later on, his brother Samuel removed to Cleveland, and in 1862 Henry followed him, and again they became partners in business. They at once took a leading position, the firm of S. C. Brooks & Co. being identified with many of the important public and private buildings. Soon after his death, which occurred June 10th, 1882, his eldest son Herbert and his grandson Henry succeeded to the business, and it is still carried on under the name of the Brooks Building Co. His wife's death followed about one year later, they leaving three sons, all of whom are married and living in this city, the eldest, Herbert, succeeding him in business; the second son, Henry, being a member of the insurance firm of Brooks, Manning & Co., and the youngest, Stephen, being a member of the publishing and stationery house of Brooks & Co.

From boyhood he was a professing Christian, and until his removal to Cleveland a member of the Presbyterian Church of Elyria, of which he was a deacon. He was also a great Sabbath school worker, being superintendent for many years of the school connected with that church.

He continued his labors in this direction on his removal to Cleveland, being superintendent of the First Congregational Sunday school for many years, and a deacon and prominent worker in the church.

NICOLAS MEYER,

born July 7th, 1809, at Niederalben, in the Bavarian Palatinate in Germany, son of Nicolas and Barbara Meyer, nee Schneider, emigrated to the United States in 1833, and arrived in Cleveland in 1834. In 1836, he married Dorothea Jacob, twelve children being the fruit of said union, seven of whom survive him.

Being by occupation a carpenter and builder, he worked at his trade about three years, when he became a contractor, and successfully continued so until 1869. In 1838 he made his first land purchase of Diodate Clark, which he sold at a fair profit in 1851, to become a part of the Jno. G. Jennings allotment on University Heights. From that time on until his death, Mr. Meyer became largely interested in various real estate transactions on the south side of the city, and by his sound judgment, close application to business and reputation for fair dealing succeeded in the acquisition of a large estate, when, in the zenith of prosperity, he was suddenly cut down by disease, and died May 23d, 1884, deplored by his wife and seven surviving children.

He was a good, conscientious Christian man, of strong character and sterling integrity, and the community lost in him a citizen who had ever assisted generously in the promotion of any measure that promised to benefit a good cause.

THOS. H. LAMSON

was born at Sheffield, Mass., July 16th, 1827. The story of his life is in a sense but a repetition of the familiar story of the straightforward, industrious, persevering Berkshire boy—his life apparently hemmed in by circumstances as hard and immovable as the hills that shut in his little home. He left the parental roof at the age of twenty, going to Southington, Conn., where he remained twenty years. That he was successful, the extensive factory of The Lamson & Sessions Co., which was moved to this city from Connecticut, in 1867, and of which he was the originator, stands to-day a monument to the well-earned and brilliant success of the firm of which he was always an honored member. During his short business career, he established a healthy public sentiment in favor of temperance, sterling integrity, justice, charity and commercial fidelity. Social and genial in his nature, his friends were many. His sympathy was great, his generosity far-reaching. After a brief illness, he died at Lenox, Mass., whither he had gone, hoping the air of his native hills might restore him to health.

Broad in his views, sincere in his religious convictions, noble and generous in his impulses, a safe counselor, a tried Christian, a public benefactor, a faithful friend, he peacefully sleeps at Riverside, our beautiful city of the dead, of which he was one of the founders.

JOSIAH BARBER

was born December 3d, 1825, at a farm located on what is known as the South Side. He was for a number of years engaged as a civil engineer, and took a prominent part in the construction of the C., C., C. & I. Railway. He was also employed in a similar capacity in the building of the L. S. & M. S. Railroad. The Bee Line curve at Delaware and the Rocky River road were constructed under the direction of Mr. Barber. He removed to Columbus in 1850, and in the following year was united in marriage to Miss Caroline J. Cooke, daughter of one of the pioneers of Franklin county. In 1862, he enlisted, at Columbus, in the 95th Regiment, O. V. I., and served with honor to the close of the war. He entered the service as a lieutenant, and retired at the close of the long struggle with the rank of captain. Mr. Barber then removed to Cleveland, and resided in this city until the time of his death. He was the first president of the Riverside Cemetery Association, and for a number of years had occupied the position of superintendent. His re-election to the position occurred only a few days before his death. Mr. Barber was a prominent member of the Army of the Tennessee, and was also identified with Memorial Post, G. A. R., No. 141, of this city.

R. F. HUMISTON

was born in Great Barrington, Mass., July 29th, 1821, and died April 4th, 1889. When he was about twelve years of age his family moved to Hudson, O., where Western Reserve College was then located, and he early became imbued with a desire to acquire more than a common school education. His mind once made up to this, it was not lost sight of, and to this end his efforts led him in various ways, now as store-boy or clerk, again to carpentry, and later on to teaching in country schools.

Before entirely completing his college course, he accepted the principalship of an academy at Cuyahoga Falls, from which, in

1848, he came to Cleveland, and was an active teacher and otherwise prominently associated with the educational interests here, for a period of twenty years, the last ten of which were at Cleveland Institute, of which he was proprietor and principal. For several years of this time, he occupied also the chair of chemistry in the Cleveland Homœopathic College. This college conferred upon him the honorary degree of M. D., as did Western Reserve of A. M.

The years of 1869 and '70 he spent abroad, during which time he took an extended course in chemistry and geology, and was made a Fellow of the Royal Chemical and Geological Societies of London, England. After his return, he gave a few years to the establishment of a colony in south-western Minnesota, since which time his business interests were mainly centered in the East.

As a teacher, he brought a rare enthusiasm to his work, well calculated to arouse deep interest and inspiration in his pupils, even among those hitherto dull and unambitious. His own early struggles gave him a ready sympathy with young men who had their own way to make, and better than that, he had the power to stimulate their courage and make noble achievement consciously possible to them. Beyond this, he has given a helping hand to many a young man who has dated the beginnings of his success to this kindness.

Till within a few weeks of his death, he was an indefatigable student and worker, and but for the overtaxing of his powers, years of health and usefulness would have seemed assured him.

JULIUS C. SCHENCK, M. D.,

was born in Cassel, Germany, February 7th, 1836. While a youth, his parents emigrated to this country. At the age of eighteen, he entered the Cleveland Medical College, from where he graduated in 1858. In 1861, he entered the service of the volunteer army as assistant surgeon of the 37th regiment, O. V. I. This position he retained one year, when he was promoted to the surgeonship of the same regimen. On his return from the field he was appointed assistant surgeon of the United States Hospital, established on the South Side during the war.

He practiced medicine in this city until his death, which occurred July 27th, 1883.

THOMAS DIXON.

Two of the promoters of Riverside Cemetry, Thomas Dixon and Dr. J. C. Schenck, had the life crushed out of them in a railroad accident in July, 1883.

Thomas Dixon was a native of Portsmouth, England, and came to this country in 1840. He first settled in Kingston, on the North river, where he married Elizabeth Krum. They came to Cleveland in 1845, where his widow and only remaining child still reside.

Mr. Dixon had a quick ear for music and was a great lover of flowers and floraculture, and was a firm believer in the life to come. Let us hope that he is now realizing the inscription upon his monument :

"Listening to the music of angels,
In the Garden of the Lord."

His friendly and genial nature made him many fast friends. He always took a lively interest in the success of the enterprise which provided him with a last resting place—Riverside Cemetery.

FRANCIS BRANCH,

son of Seth and Rachel (Hurd) Branch, was born on the 5th of June, 1812, at Middle Haddam, Conn. His father, Seth Branch, was a native of the same place, having been born on the 31st of March, 1779, and having been married in 1805 to Rachel Hurd. He removed to Ohio in 1818 and settled on what is now known as Brooklyn Heights, Cleveland. There were but few houses in the neighborhood at that time and Mr. Branch was fortunate in securing shelter for his family in the home of Judge Barber until a dwelling could be erected. He died on the 11th of August, 1825, at the premature age of 46, leaving as a legacy to his family only their home in the forest and a name respected by all. Francis Branch remained at home until the death of his father, after which he was apprenticed to a ship carpenter; John, his eldest brother, taking charge of the farm. He followed his trade until 1837. In that year he was married to Sarah Slaght, daughter of Abram D. Slaght, and his brother dying, he soon afterward removed to the homestead. He then engaged in agriculture and dairying, meeting with fair success in both. He was also one of the first milk sellers in that locality, and after a time carried on quite an extensive traffic in that line.

In 1850, Mr. Branch sold the farm, which had become quite valuable, and in May, 1851, removed to a residence on Scranton avenue, where he lived until his death, which occurred on the 4th of November, 1877.

Mr. Branch was a self-made man; losing his father when only fourteen years old, he was thus thrown on his own resources, and with a limited education acquired a fortune and won an honorable place in the community.

He held various township offices, besides serving three terms as county commissioner.

In public improvements, he always took an active interest, and was a liberal contributor to all local enterprises.

Throughout life he maintained a high character for integrity and honor, while his many excellent qualities and unassuming manners won the respect of all. He left one child, Mrs. Josephine S. Hartzell.

DR. A. G. SPRINGSTEEN

was born in New York City, December 10th, 1827. He received his early education mainly in that city. But he was a man who recognized the fact that no person was ever fully educated, and with added years he industriously added to his knowledge, down to his demise. With the acquisition of knowledge in view, he, when a young physician, spent some time in the West Indies and in Central America.

Dr. Springsteen was united in marriage at Whiting's point, New York, July 4th, 1856, with Miss Helen Pritchard, who survives him.

At the annual meeting of the National Eclectic Medical Association, held in the city of New York, in October, 1871, he was elected a permanent member of that association. He was later vice-president of the same association. He was also a member of the Ohio State Eclectic Medical Association, having been elected May 23, 1877.

He was a graduate of the National Eclectic Medical College of New York City, in 1854. He also received a diploma from the United States Medical College, (Eclectic), of New York City, in 1881. He was a man of literary taste and ability.

For a few years he was editor-in-chief of an influential newspaper published at Rockford, Ill. Before the exactions of his profession so largely required his attention, he wrote, as he could spare the time, articles for magazines and newspapers, and delivered public addresses on subjects connected with his profession. Among the latter was one highly prized, delivered before the officers and inmates of Bellevue Hospital, New York, and invited spectators. Dr. Springsteen became an honorary member of the organization of the 124th Regiment O. V. I., at the regular reunion held at the Eighteenth Ward, (Newburgh), of Cleveland, September 19th, 1877. And though he was not enrolled as a soldier during the late war, he was deputed by the authorities on important business within our lines in some of the states in insurrection and successfully performed his mission. He was genial in his ways and entertaining. Few men more enjoyed extending hospitalities to their associates. He had a happy faculty of making friends and attaching them to him. He numbered among them men not only of national reputation, but by their official capacity, well known in Europe. By his natural talents, learning, acute theory of medicines and faithful and conscientious attention to those requiring his medical services he had built in Cleveland an enviable practice on a firm foundation.

Many there are, who losing his professional ministrations, join with other friends in sincerely mourning his loss. On the 16th of July, 1882—midsummer—and when it would seem that he was at mid-life of activity and usefulness, as the sun was nearing the horizon, his spirit took its departure from its earthly tenement.

"Life's fitful fever o'er, he sleeps well."

CHARLES SHERMAN COFFINBERRY,

whose earthly remains rest within these lovely grounds, was born in Mansfield, Ohio, February 1st, 1824, and died at Atherton's ranch, near Pueblo, Colo., December 17th, 1873. He was the son of Andrew Coffinberry and brother of Judge J. M. Coffinberry. He read law with his father in Perrysburg, O., and was admitted to the bar in 1842, and practiced his profession in Findlay, in company with John H. Morrison, until the memorable year of 1849, when, with the moving tide, he crossed the continent to California. Under the appointment of President Fillmore, he took the first census of California, and for a time was deputy clerk of the Supreme and Common Pleas Courts in Naffa county.

'e was for a time associated profession-
Returning to Clevelan(but failing health impelled him to
ally with Judge Coffinberi, -mong the mountains of the South-
seek in travel more genial air a for gold. He was eminent-
west. He sought for health more than ~ honest and honorable
ly social and friendly, and lived and died an .
man.

A. C. GETCHELL

[.] At was a native of Maine, born at Waterville. March 8th, 182. and the age of 12 years he shipped on board a vessel at Boston .f visited England, India, Japan, China and the western coast o. America. In 1848, he was married to Caroline E. Q. Norton. of Portland, Maine. He took up his residence in our city thirty-six years ago. He died September 7th. 1888, leaving a wife and two children to survive him.

THE LATE MARION E. BECKWITH,

who died at his residence, Tuesday. December 13, 1887. was one of Cleveland's pioneers, and a man widely loved and honored. He was born in Erie county, New York. on November 4th, 1823, and came to Cleveland December 16, 1839. He was married on January 23, 1845, to Miss Margaret McLeod, daughter of the late General D. McLeod, who survives him. During the almost half century of his residence in this city, he has been a typical good citizen, a man of the highest integrity, owner of a kind and generous heart, and possessed of a pure and noble character. He won his place in the business world by strict integrity, industry and fair dealing. His connection with the photographic business has been long and progressive.

He suffered intensely with cancer, yet he never complained, and while lying upon his death-bed he quietly made all arrangements for his funeral, selecting the spot in Riverside where he desired to be buried. When his arrangements had been made, Mr. Beckwith went out with the tide, peacefully and calmly, caressing the face of his dearly beloved wife and expressing the hope that, when her earthly pilgrimage was ended, they might journey on together through eternity, as they had journeyed through life.

STEPHEN WOOD

was born at Gravesend, a famous old commercial city on the Thames, county of Kent, England, March 15, 1818. His father was a carpenter and placed his son as an apprentice to a mason. After acquiring the trade, he, in 1847, came to the United States and settled in Hudson, N. Y. One year after, he followed the course of empire and came to Clevelend. Here he became a mason contractor, which business he followed till 1867, when he made sewering a specialty, and soon thereafter and until his death the firm name of S. Wood & Sons was familiar throughout the city.

Mr. Wood died August 22d, 1880. His beloved wife was laid beside him seven years later. In a pleasant nook, surrounded by trees, on the south road of Riverside, their mortal remains rest. A beautiful granite monument marks the ever quiet spot, and whither are often seen their children Henry, James, Walter, Charles, Thomas and Jane, with their tribute of flowers to bedeck the graves of their beloved parents.

DIODATE CLARK,

who died at his home in this city, on Monday, September 4th, 1876, had resided here since 1817. He was born September 19th, 1798, in Haddam, Connecticut. His parents being poor, and having nine children, young Diodate was bound out at the age of ten years, and worked on a farm near Springfield, Mass., for several years. At the age of nineteen he and his brother Kelly started on foot for the West. His brother gave out and returned, but Diodate kept on, and landed in Cleveland with his bundle of clothes in his knap-sack, having only one dollar left. He at once found work in chopping and clearing land, Cleveland being then only a small village in the midst of the forest. Such enterprise and resolution soon enabled him to buy a farm in what was then the township of Brooklyn. He added to his land until he had a farm of over 200 acres, which has long since made a part of the city by its rapid growth. His sagacity and sound judgment, his success in business and unquestioned integrity, gave him a place as one of the leading citizens of the county, and for at least four terms he served the county as one of its commissioners.

He was one of the first to commence the manufacture of lime in this city, having at different times many kilns about the city. He invested in vessel property, and was long identified with the commercial interests of the city. More recently he has been a stockholder and chief manager in the different companies for the manufacture of woodenware.

Such were his qualities of character and his promptness in all his engagements, that he established a confidence in his name such as but few business men are able to achieve.

In 1828, he enrolled his name with a small number of Methodists, who met for class weekly and held services in the court house, which was then standing on the north-west corner of the now Monument Square. In 1835, he was a trustee and assisted in the building of what was subsequently known as Hanover Street Methodist Church, on the West Side. Soon after removing to his late residence, on Columbus street, he joined the Methodist Society in Brooklyn, holding his membership with them for about thirty years. For the last twelve years he has been a member of the Franklin Street Methodist Church. His wise counsel, as one of its trustees, and his liberal gifts contributed in no small measure to the erection of their present beautiful edifice.

In 1822, he was married to Caroline Aiken. Three children were born to this union, two of whom survive, and are now living in this city—Mrs. George W. Calkins and Mrs. Caroline Kellogg. His wife dying in 1828, he was married in 1829 to Sarah White Lindsley. His second wife having died in 1863, he was in 1864 married to Mrs. Samuel Tyler.

LEVI SARGENT.

The subject of this sketch was one of the stalwart few who laid deep and strong the foundations of the city of Cleveland. Born in Sanbornton, New Hampshire, September 21st, 1777, during the darkest days of the struggle of our country for independence, his youth was the youth of the country. He fitted himself for usefulness by learning the trade of a blacksmith, and set up business for himself in the township of Plumfield, in his native State, and in 1804 married Rosamond B. Harris. In the midst of our last war with Great Britain they moved to the frontier in the State of New York, "the Genesee country," and in 1817 pushed forward across Lake Erie to the "River Raisin"—Michigan. The following year they retraced their steps to Cleveland, and in 1819 settled down for life on the west side of the Cuyahoga, then Brooklyn township, with a family of five children, all of whom survive them, and at the time of this writing, 1882, still live. Mr. Sargent pressed his vocation on the West Side until, soon after the Ohio Canal was completed he built for the times, a large ship on the canal basin, near South Water street, and did a large business in ship and canal boat smithing, until age granted him a furlough.

Honesty and probity, industry and frugality were characteristics of his life work. The latter years of Levi and Rosamond B. Sargent were quietly spent in the families of their loving daughters.

Rosamond B. Sargent was a faithful co-worker in the household to train aright, and, so far as the means of the country would admit, educate their children and direct them in the ways of truth and virtue. She was a faithful and earnest friend to the poor, and a hearty and constant laborer in founding and establishing Trinity and St. John's Episcopal Churches, under the lead of the venerable and venerated Bishop Chase.

Not content with the scanty means the county afforded for school training, under great self-denial, she took her oldest son—the writer of this sketch—in the dead of Winter, in a farmer's sled, to her father in New Hampshire, seven hundred miles, and left him there for ten years to acquire knowledge unattainable on the frontier. They both lived and died in Cleveland, at the ripe age of four-score and four, with the love and honor of all who knew them as unperishable as the granite rock on which their monument stands in Riverside Cemetery.

ROBERT PRESCOTT

was born in Somersetshire, England, November 5th, 1822, and was married in 1847 to Miss Mary Webber. To them was born a son, William. His wife died in 1851. In 1853, he married Ann Fulford and came at once to America, settling on University Heights, where he continued to reside until his death on June 6th, 1889, he then being in his sixty-seventh year. To within some fifteen years prior to his death he followed his chosen occupation, that of a mason and builder. He inherited from his mother an asthmatic tendency, that developed with age, and the last years of his life were intermingled with great suffering as a consequence. He was a patient sufferer—and at all times one of those honorable, straight forward, whole-souled, genial men whose friends were many and whose loss is keenly felt. His widow and son survive him.

AFTER DEATH IN ARABIA.

BY EDWIN ARNOLD.

He who died at Azan sends
This to comfort all his friends.

Faithful friends! It lies, I know,
Pale and white and cold as snow;
And ye say, "Abdallah's dead!"
Weeping at the feet and head.
I can see your falling tears,
I can hear your sighs and prayers;
Yet I smile and whisper this—
"*I* am not the thing you kiss;
Cease your tears and let it lie;
It *was* mine, it is not I."

Sweet friends! What the women lave
For its last bed of the grave,
Is but a hut which I am quitting,
Is a garment no more fitting,
Is a cage from which at last,
Like a hawk my soul hath passed
Love the inmate, not the room—
The wearer, not the garb—the plume
Of the falcon, not the bars
Which kept him from those splendid stars.

Loving friends! Be wise and dry
Straightway every weeping eye,—
What ye lift upon the bier
Is not worth a wistful tear.
'Tis an empty sea-shell—one
Out of which the pearl is gone;
The shell is broken, it lies there;
The pearl, the all, the soul is here.
'Tis an earthen jar, whose lid
Allah sealed, the while it hid
That treasure of his treasury,
A mind that loved him: let it lie!
Let the shard be earth's once more,
Since the gold shines in his store!

Allah glorious! Allah good!
Now thy world is understood;
Now the long, long wonder ends;
Yet ye weep, my erring friends,
While the man whom ye call dead,
In unspoken bliss instead,
Lives and loves you; lost, 'tis true,
By such light as shines for you;
But in the light ye cannot see
Of unfulfilled felicity,—
In enlarging paradise,
Lives a life that never dies.

Farewell, friends! Yet not farewell;
Where I am, ye too shall dwell.
I am gone before your face,
A moment's time, a little space.
When ye come where I have stepped
Ye will wonder why ye wept;
Ye will know by wise love taught,

That here is all and there is naught.
Weep awhile, if ye are fain,—
Sunshine still must follow rain;
Only not at death—for death,
Now I know, is that first breath
Which our souls draw when we enter
Life, which is of all life center.

Be ye certain all seems love,
Viewed from Allah's throne above;
Be ye stout of heart and come
Bravely onward to your home!
La Allah, illa Allah! yea!
Thou love divine! Thou love alway!

He that died at Azan gave
This to those who made his grave.

www.ingramcontent.com/pod-product-compliance
Lightning Source LLC
Chambersburg PA
CBHW020154170426
43199CB00010B/1027